SEVEN MILES OF STEEL THISTLES

Reflections on Fairy Tales

Katherine Langrish's fiction titles:

TROLL FELL

TROLL MILL

TROLL BLOOD

DARK ANGELS

FORSAKEN

SEVEN MILES OF STEEL THISTLES

Reflections on Fairy Tales

KATHERINE LANGRISH

'There are seven miles of hill on fire for you to cross, and there are seven miles of steel thistles, and seven miles of sea.'

The Greystones Press

First published in Great Britain in 2016 by

The Greystones Press Ltd
Greystones
37 Lawton Avenue
Carterton
Oxfordshire OX18 3JY

A CIP catalogue record for this book is available from the British Library

PB ISBN: 978-1-911122-04-3
EBOOK ISBN: 978-1-911122-05-0

1 3 5 7 9 10 8 6 4 2

Designed and typeset by Nigel Hazle

Printed in Great Britain by Clays Ltd, St Ives plc

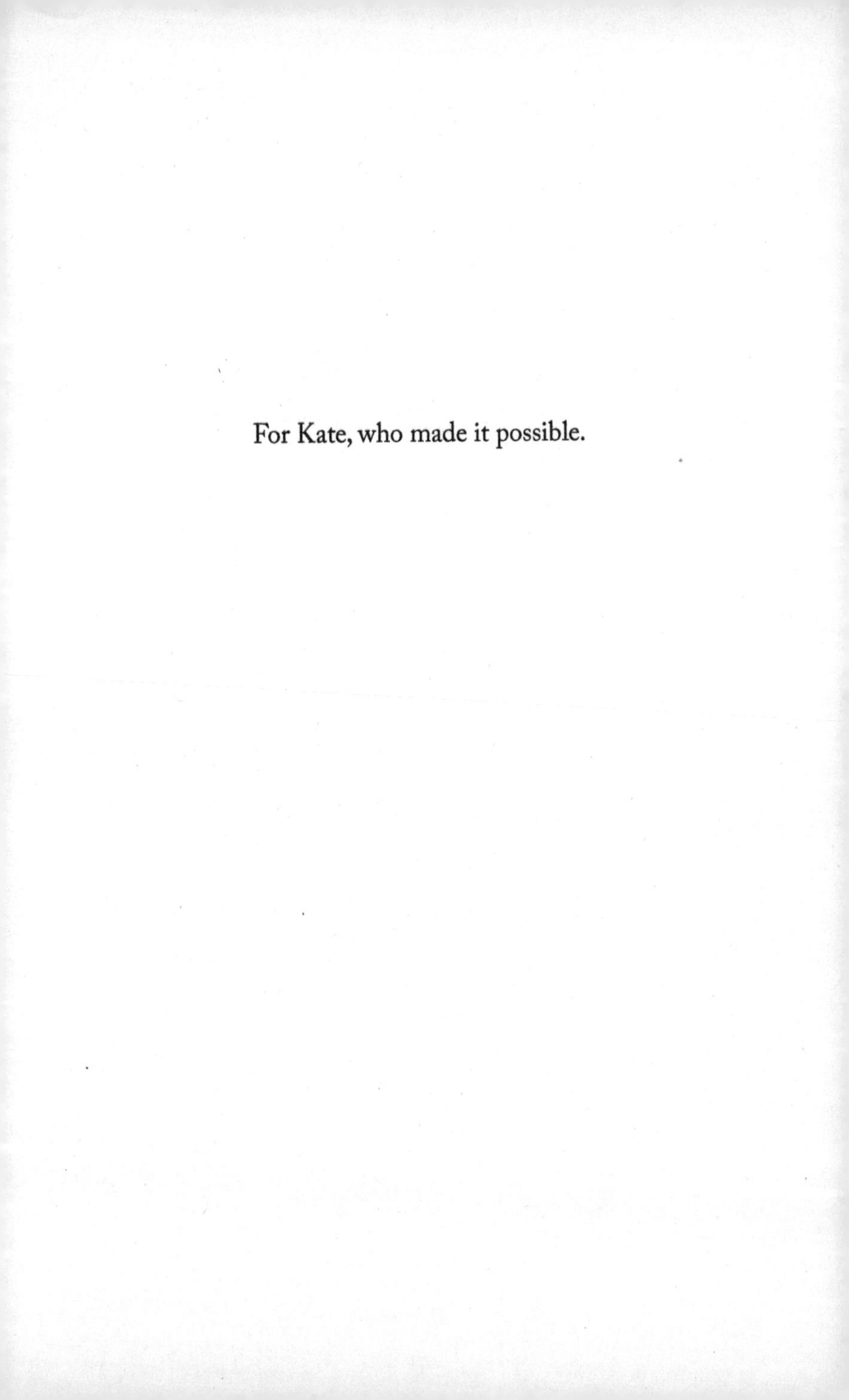

For Kate, who made it possible.

Contents

Reflections on Folk Tales

Envoi

On Fairy Tales

Introduction

As I write, it is eight years since I founded a blog on all things to do with fairy tales, folklore, fantasy and children's literature, and named it 'Seven Miles of Steel Thistles' – a phrase I borrowed from an Irish fairy tale in which the hero gallops his pony over 'seven miles of hill on fire, and seven miles of steel thistles, and seven miles of sea'. I am a children's author by trade and by vocation, and I thought this strong image was a good metaphor for what sometimes feel like the insuperable difficulties of writing a book. Or of life in general, for that matter.

The blog flourished. Through it I met many new friends who shared my belief that fairy tales are worth reading and worth studying, and that the capacity to imagine things that *don't exist* is one of the most important human traits. A blog is an ephemeral thing, however. Day by day, week by week, posts disappear from view like falling leaves, and who goes looking for them again? A post is also, by its nature, short – often there simply isn't room to say everything you want to say. Though many of the essays in this book had their origin on my blog,

I've revised and extended all of them and learned a lot in the process. Some have changed beyond recognition. It's been fun.

I've loved fairy tales all my life. I was lucky enough to grow up in a house crammed with books and can't remember learning to read; it seemed something I was born doing. As a child I was usually deep in a book, and as often as not, it would be full of fairy tales or myths and legends from around the world. I remember choosing the Norse myths for a school project, retelling and illustrating stories about Thor, Odin and Loki. I read the tales of King Arthur, I read stories from the Arabian Nights. And gradually, I hardly know how, I became aware that grown-ups made distinctions between these, to me, very similar genres. Some were taken more seriously than others. Myths – specifically the 'Greek myths' – were top of the list and legends came second, while fairy tales were the poor cousins at the bottom. Yet there appeared to be a considerable overlap. Andrew Lang included the story of Perseus and Andromeda in *The Blue Fairy Book*, under the title 'The Terrible Head'. And surely he was right: it *is* a fairy tale, about a prince who rescues a princess from a monster! In a story book[1] handed down from my mother I read three tales by Nathaniel Hawthorne: 'The Inquisitive Girl', 'The Golden Touch' and 'The Pomegranate Seeds'. These were retellings of the myths of Pandora, King Midas and Proserpina, but they were indistinguishable from fairy tales.

The field of fairy stories, legends, folk tales and myths is like a great, wild meadow. The flowers and grasses seed everywhere;

---

1 *The Mammoth Wonder Book*, ed. John R. Crossland & J.M. Parrish.

boundaries are impossible to maintain. Wheat grows into the hedge from the cultivated fields nearby, and poppies spring up in the middle of the oats. A story can be both things at once, a 'Greek myth' and a fairy tale too: but if we're going to talk about them, broad distinctions can still be made and may still be useful. Here is what I think: a *myth* seeks to make emotional sense of the world and our place in it. Thus, the story of Persephone's abduction by Hades is a religious and poetic exploration of winter and summer, death and rebirth. A *legend* recounts the deeds of heroes, such as Achilles, Arthur or Cú Chulainn. A *folk tale* is a humbler, more local affair. Its protagonists may be well-known neighbourhood characters or they may be anonymous, but specific *places* become important. Folk narratives occur in real, named landscapes. Green fairy children are found near the village of Woolpit in Suffolk.[2] A Cheshire farmer going to market to sell a white mare meets a wizard, not just anywhere, but on Alderley Edge between Mobberley and Macclesfield.[3] In Dorset an ex-soldier called John Lawrence sees a phantom army marching 'from the direction of Flowers Barrow, over Grange Hill, and making for Wareham'.[4] Local hills, lakes, stones and even churches are explained as the work of giants, trolls or the Devil.

Fairy tales can be divided into literary tales, the more-or-less original work of authors such as Hans Christian Andersen, George MacDonald and Oscar Wilde (which will not concern

---

2 Keightley, Thomas, *The Fairy Mythology*, 281.

3 Axon, William, *Cheshire Gleanings*, 56 et seq (and made famous by Alan Garner).

4 Marshall, Sybil, *Everyman's Book of English Folk Tales*, 164.

me very much in this book), and anonymous traditional tales, originally handed down the generations by word of mouth but nowadays usually mediated to us via print. Unlike folk tales, traditional fairy tales are usually set 'far away and long ago' and lack temporal and spatial reference points. They begin like this: 'In olden times, when wishing still helped one, there lived a king . . .' or else, 'A long time ago there was a king who was famed for his wisdom through all the land . . .' A hero goes travelling, and 'after he had travelled some days, he came one night to a Giant's house . . .' We are everywhere or nowhere, never somewhere. A fairy tale is universal, not local.

Characters in fairy tales rarely possess names: when they do, these are either descriptive, like 'Little Red-Cap' and 'Snow-White', or else extremely common, such as Gretel, Hans, Kate, Jack. The effect is inclusive: these are the adventures of Everyman and Everywoman, but most of the time fairy-tale characters are referred to even more generically, as 'the king's daughter', 'the boy', 'the maiden', 'the soldier', 'the tailor' and so on.

None of the traditional forms – myth, legend, folk or fairy tale – can or should be approached in the same way that we approach a novel. They are not, for example, the least little bit interested in building characters' inner lives. Fairy-tale characters are established briefly, succinctly and once for all: 'a dear little girl', 'a poor old woman', 'two daughters, one ugly and wicked, the other beautiful and good'. That's it, set in stone. They won't develop or change, and everything that happens to them happens on the outside. Again, though fairy-tale narratives operate perfectly well by their own sets of rules (the third son is the lucky one; kindness to an animal wins you a magical helper), these are not the rules we expect from a novel. At the beginning of her story, Snow-White is a child of seven. By the end, she marries the prince. So . . . how old is she now? How long did she keep house for the dwarfs; how long has she lain in the glass coffin? Is this a lingering memory of some dark practice of child brides? It's a mistake to ask. It's a category error to look for that kind of consistency in a fairy tale. Snow-White is old enough to marry the prince at the end of the story for no other reason than that the narrative demands she should be. *That is how the story ends.*

Plenty of traditional fairy tales contain no actual fairies at all. (Unless you count the dwarfs, there are none in *Little Snow-White*, for example.) The term 'fairy tale' seems to have originated with Madame d'Aulnoy's *Les Contes de Fées* or 'Tales of the Fairies', published in 1697. According to the well-known fairy-tale scholar Jack Zipes, 'By the time of her death a few years later . . . d'Aulnoy's name had become synonymous with an expression she was the first to use – *contes de fées*.'[5] Madame d'Aulnoy's sophisticated, literary, fanciful stories feature characters such as the amiable Fairy Gentille or the wicked Fairy Carabosse, who help or harm the fortunes of pairs of delightful young lovers. The magic in these tales is consciously amusing: in *The Blue Bird*, for example, King Charming rides in a chariot drawn by winged frogs, and shouts, 'My frogs! My frogs!' when he wishes to depart.[6] Good and bad fairies make

---

5 Zipes, Jack, *The Oxford Companion to Fairy Tales*, 33.
6 D'Aulnoy, Madame, *The Fairy Tales of Madame d'Aulnoy*, tr. Anne Thackeray Ritchie, 38.

appearances in many of Charles Perrault's tales (also published in 1697, a good year for the genre) but certainly not in all: there are none in *Little Red Riding Hood* or *Bluebeard*, for example. Perhaps reflecting this, Perrault's collection is called simply *Histoires ou contes du temps passé*, 'Stories or tales of long ago'. And in 1810 Jacob and Wilhelm Grimm, whose interest was in the origins of traditional German tales, gave to their own collection the unassuming title *Kinder- und Hausmärchen*, 'Children's and Household Tales'. There are fewer fairies to be found in the Grimms' tales than there are witches and wicked stepmothers, but English translations persist in calling them 'fairy' tales. And why not? It's what we've grown used to.

Of course, the Grimm brothers were an inspirational part of the great Europe-wide revival of interest in traditional tales that sprang up as part of the Romantic movement and of nascent nationalism. They set the standard for many other collectors throughout the nineteenth century and into the twentieth.[7] The world became a wilder, more magical place. Selkies plunged through the wild waves beyond Orkney. Undines drew themselves sinuously out of German rivers. The Neckan plucked his harp and sang mournfully on Scandinavian headlands and Baba Yaga flew through the Russian forests in her pestle and mortar to light down at her skull-bedecked garden gate.

---

7 Such as Ireland's Thomas Crofton Croker, William Larminie, Thomas Keightley, Lady Augusta Gregory and William Butler Yeats, Norway's Peter Christen Asbjornsen and Jorgen Moe, Britain's Sir George Dasent, Andrew Lang, Sir William Craigie and Joseph Jacobs (who was actually Australian), and Russia's Aleksandr Afanasyev.

At first, such stories were collected by adults and intended for adults. Sir George Webbe Dasent specifically forbids 'good children' to read the last two (mildly naughty) tales in *Popular Tales from the Norse*, his 1859 translation of Asbjornsen and Moe's *Norske Folkeeventyr.*[8] Referring to himself in the third person, he writes:

> He will never know if any bad child has broken his behest. Still he hopes that all good children who read this book will bear in mind that there is just as much sin in breaking a commandment even though it not be found out, and so he bids them goodbye, and feels sure that no good child will dare to look into those two rooms. If, after this warning, they peep in, they may find something that will shock them.
>
> 'Why then print them at all?' some grown reader asks. Because this volume is meant for you as well as for children, and if you have gone ever so little into the world with open eyes, you must have seen, yes, every day, things much more shocking.[9]

Concern for children's morals was to exercise many an editor in the decades to follow, most of whom trusted to censorship rather than simple appeals to honour. In 1889

---

8 Published in Norway, 1841.

9 Dasent, Sir George, *Popular Tales from the Norse*, vi.

Andrew Lang published *The Blue Fairy Book*, the first in his immensely successful series known as 'the Colour Fairy Books'. Actually his wife Leonora Blanche Alleyne, whom he credits in *The Lilac Fairy Book*, was 'almost wholly' responsible for the selections and translations. Compiled specifically for children, they were collections of stories, both literary and traditional, from many different countries and cultures, lightly bowdlerised where necessary. Parents could be confident in their suitability, and children liked them because Mrs Lang's choices were excellent and she didn't preach. Lang struck hard at the 'new' fairy tales then being churned out for children's consumption:

> The three hundred and sixty-five authors who try to write new fairy tales are very tiresome. They always begin with a little boy or girl who goes out and meets the fairies of polyanthuses and gardenias and apple blossoms: 'Flowers and fruits and other winged things.' These fairies try to be funny, and fail, or they try to preach, and succeed. Real fairies never preach or talk slang. At the end, the little boy or girl wakes up and finds that he has been dreaming.[10]

Coincidentally, 1889 was also the year in which Lewis Carroll published *Sylvie and Bruno*, a book which most people now find unreadable. In it, Carroll also took time to have a go at

---

10 Lang, Andrew, *The Lilac Fairy Book*, viii.

the moralising tone of late nineteenth-century children's fairy fiction:

> I want to know – dear Child who reads this! – why Fairies should always be teaching *us* to do our duty, and lecturing *us* when we go wrong, and we should never teach *them* anything?[11]

But he didn't manage to avoid the pitfalls himself. We soon meet two tiny fairies, who are simply miniature children. Good little Sylvie is trying to turn over a big beetle struggling on his back: 'it was as much as she could do, with both arms, to roll the heavy thing over; and all the while she was talking to it, half scolding and half comforting, as a nurse might do with a child that had fallen down'. In contrast to kind Sylvie we next encounter naughty Bruno, who is busy tearing up Sylvie's garden.

> Think of any pretty little boy you know, with rosy cheeks, large, dark eyes and tangled brown hair, and then fancy him made small enough to fit comfortably into a coffee cup . . .[12]

Bruno speaks in the lisping baby-talk which Victorian writers found so inexplicably appealing. 'Revenge is a wicked, cruel, dangerous thing', Carroll-as-narrator tells the little fairy.

---

11 Carroll, Lewis, *Sylvie and Bruno*, 190.
12 Op. cit., 198.

'River-edge?' Bruno responds. 'What a funny word! I suppose oo call it cruel and dangerous 'cause, if oo wented too far and tumbleded in, oo'd get drownded.' This illustrates how difficult it must have been for Victorians to avoid gluey sentiment when writing about fairies for children. Even the creator of Alice couldn't escape it! To return to *The Blue Fairy Book* after this kind of thing is like striding out into open country and wild winds, and to realise what a great service the Langs did for nineteenth-century children.

And though Lang may have suppressed hints of immoral behaviour in fairy tales, he was bracing in his attitudes to violence. It was in *The Blue Fairy Book* that I first read the full version of Perrault's *The Sleeping Beauty in the Wood*, with its thrillingly gruesome second half – these days usually forgotten – in which the King's ogress mother orders the young Queen and both her little children to be killed and cooked with *sauce Robert* (whatever that was). After a last-minute rescue, the wicked ogress is thrown into a pit full of toads and vipers. It was not for the faint-hearted. Whether the two halves of the story truly belong together or no, I loved it, and I appreciated its touches of macabre humour: the Sleeping Beauty may *look* young but she is actually a hundred and twenty, so 'her flesh must be expected to be on the tough side'. My local library stocked all of the Colour Fairy Books: Blue, Red, Green, Crimson, Yellow, Brown, Lilac, Violet . . . I read the lot. I read everything else, too, but fairy tales were a staple of my diet.

You couldn't exhaust them; they were all so different. Some were quirky and funny, like *Puss in Boots*. Some, especially French stories like *The White Cat* or *Beauty and the Beast*, felt bright and light and pretty. The Grimms' tales were dark and scary. Hans Christian Andersen's stories were beautifully, deliciously sad. The poor little Mermaid! The poor little Match Girl! The poor little Fir-Tree! And sometimes they were horrifying, like *The Red Shoes*, the story of the vain girl whose red shoes dance her away without stopping, until she has to have both her feet chopped off by a woodcutter. I was about eight years old when I first read it, and unfortunately my mother had just bought me a pair of red leather shoes, which from then on I absolutely refused to wear.

If traditional fairy tales could be strong meat, in other children's books I still met plenty of the soppy fairies so despised by Andrew Lang – fragile little creatures who danced on tiptoe, lived in flowers or under toadstools, and wore bluebell hats. I didn't altogether mind them, but compared with real fairy tales, they were pretty tame. A good example is *Pink Paint for a Pixie*, a story by Enid Blyton in which a little girl loans her paintbox to a pixie and is rewarded when he paints the tips of the daisies pink so that she can make a magical necklace.[13] Twentieth-century fairies had ceased to preach, but they were always *helpful*: not for nothing did Lady Baden-Powell name her girl scout movement 'the Brownies' – after an earlier name, 'the Rosebuds', proved unpopular with girls. Brownies were presented as helpful domestic sprites (most unlike the unpredictable tricksters of folklore), and the traditional names for the Brownie 'sixes' when I joined briefly

---

13 Blyton, Enid, 'Pink Paint for a Pixie', *A Story-Party At Green Hedges*, 106.

in the 1960s were Pixies, Elves, Leprechauns, Gnomes, Fairies and Sprites. Prejudice was rife – no one wanted to be a gnome – there were badges for feminine tasks such as knitting, sewing, and baking buns, and I left after a few weeks, partly because I did not believe I would ever learn to skip a hundred times backwards.

When I was about ten I discovered Alan Garner, who had burst upon the scene in 1960, raiding Celtic and Norse legends and throwing the booty together in the most electrifying way in his first book, *The Weirdstone of Brisingamen*. Here, and in its sequel, *The Moon of Gomrath*, two contemporary and quite conventional children – who might easily in other hands have seen fairies at the bottom of the garden – are hurled into a maelstrom of ancient magic, moon goddesses, shapeless terrors and hints of deeper worlds. A flood of magic from legend and folklore was released into children's fiction, changing it forever. There are no obvious fairies in the books; the male supernatural characters consist of a wizard, some rather chilly elves, and dwarfs: but Angharad Goldenhand, the lady of the lake, is a fairy queen in the style of the *Mabinogion* or the *Morte d'Arthur*, while her adversary the Morrigan is a witch-queen or crone worthy of Grimm. Yes, these characters are primarily intended to be perceived as aspects of the triple moon goddess, but that's what all fairy queens in folklore and ballads may once have been. And fairies in folklore have always been connected with sex as well as death:

> 'Harp and carp, Thomas,' she said
> 'Harp and carp along with me,

And if you dare to kiss my lips.
Sure of your body I will be."[14]

So Thomas the Rhymer kissed the Queen of Elphame under the Eildon Tree and rode away with her through the river of blood into elfland. Wild Edric lost his fairy wife Godda and rides for ever on the Shropshire hills with his Hunt, searching for her. As for the sexy, beautiful, dangerous male faeries of modern teen novels, they find a traditional antecedent in the Irish *Gancanagh*, the 'Love-Talker', a beautiful fairy youth who waylays young girls in the gloaming and makes them so love-sick for him that they pine away and die.

The Irish have always remembered the dangerous side of the fairies. William Allingham's fairies in *Up the Aery Mountain, Down the Rushy Glen*, with its 'Wee folk, good folk, Trooping all together, Green jacket, red cap, And white owl's feather', may fleetingly sound like Walt Disney's dwarfs. But Allingham knew the connection of the fairies with loss and death:

They stole little Bridget
For seven years long,
And when she came down again
Her friends were all gone.

They took her lightly back,
Between the night and morrow,

14 'Thomas the Rhymer', *The Oxford Book of Ballads*, ed. James Kinsley, 7 et seq.

They thought she was fast asleep,
But she was dead from sorrow.

Scottish J.M. Barrie's *Peter Pan* may have given us Tinkerbell, but his second take on a supernaturally extended youth is an eerie play about a girl stolen by the fairies, *Mary Rose*, and it doesn't have a happy ending.

The variant spelling 'faerie' has recently almost entirely replaced 'fairy' in children's and young adult fantasy fiction, probably in an effort to distinguish the human-sized, dangerous fairies of the Celtic tradition from the diminutive milk-and-water flower fairies of late nineteenth- and early twentieth-century children's fiction. Spelt 'faerie', the word somehow just *looks* more magical, too – more romantic, more grown-up, more literary – conjuring 'magic casements opening on the foam/Of perilous seas, in faerie lands forlorn . . .'[15] Fairies, faeries, elves, whatever you like to call them, symbolise bereavement and death as well as the lure of love and beauty. That's surely why the ballads divide the 'high' fairies into two 'courts': the 'Seelie Court' and the 'Unseelie Court', representing their benevolent and harmful aspects. European fairy culture is rich and complex. No wonder so many modern fantasy writers plunder it.

But let's forget the ballads and romances and the heroic Celtic legends, and look once again at the humble fairy tale. People who dislike fairy tales (and probably seldom read them) complain that at best they are romantic trivia, at worst

---

15 Keats, John, *Ode to a Nightingale*, l. 69, 70.

escapist nonsense with a side-order of sexism. Aren't they all about princes rescuing passive princesses from dragons, giants and towers? How can any self-respecting adult defend that? If it were true, perhaps I couldn't, but it is simply not so. The Grimms' tales alone include many more stories about peasants and tradesmen, farmers, beggars and pensioned-off soldiers than they do about princesses and queens. And if you think about it for a moment, the world is still full of peasants and tradesmen and farmers and beggars and pensioned-off soldiers. Just as it always was.

Hansel and Gretel is, as Adèle Geras has succinctly put it, 'about hunger' – about the terrible choices people have to face when they are at starvation's door. *The Blue Light* is about a soldier who's done his duty by his country only to be discarded and marginalised and left to tramp the roads. *The Seven Little Kids* is about a single, working mother who has to leave her children alone in the house, knowing they may be in danger. (Yes, she happens to be a goat.) *The Fisherman and his Wife* is about greed (and a poisonous marriage). *The Mouse, the Bird and The Sausage* is a cautionary tale about the dangers of blind trust and naïvety. There's even a far-fetched yarn about organ transplants called *The Three Army Surgeons*.

As Alison Lurie has said, fairy tales are much more realistic than you might think:

> To succeed in this world you needed some special skill or patronage, plus remarkable luck; and it didn't hurt to be very good looking. The other qualities that counted were wit, boldness,

> stubborn persistence and an eye to the main chance. Kindness to those in trouble was also advisable – you never knew who might be useful to you later on.[16]

Comical, tragic, beautiful or cruel, these anonymous stories are amazingly diverse and amazingly hardy. They've been told and retold, loved and laughed at, by generation after generation, because they are of the people, by the people, for the people. The world of fairy tales is one in which the pain and deprivation, bad luck and hard work of ordinary folk can be alleviated by a chance meeting, by luck, by courtesy, courage and quick wits – and by the occasional miracle. The world of fairy tales is not so very different from ours. It *is* ours.

---

16 Lurie, Alison, *Don't Tell The Grown-Ups*, 18.

Fairy brides (and bridegrooms)

A rough Hebridean fisherman spies on seal maidens dancing on a wave-battered moonlit beach. Astray in wild mountains, a Saxon lord discovers a house shining with lights and a 'great dance' of fairy women going on inside. A Japanese traveller on a dark road meets an elegant girl whose white fox tail peeps from under the hem of her robe. A young cattle herder sees a lovely lady gliding over the waters of a remote Welsh lake.

Across the world, centuries beyond reckoning, people have been telling stories about marriages, meetings, love affairs and abductions between mortals and fairies, or shape-shifting animals such as selkies, kitsune or swan-maidens. Maybe the animal spirits were once ancestral totems associated with tabus and *geasa*, such as the *geas* laid upon the Irish King Conaire never to shoot a bird:

> [His mother] saw a Bird on the skylight coming to her, and he leaves his birdskin on the floor of the house, and went to her and possessed her, and

said: '. . . Thou wilt be pregnant by me, and bear a son, and that son must not kill birds.'[1]

To have fairy blood in the family could be a matter of pride – Richard Coeur de Lion boasted his descent from the fairy Melusina who married into the house of Lusignan, and the Physicians of Myddvai derived their medical knowledge from their fairy mother the Lady of Llyn y Fan Fach. But if you are contemplating a fairy marriage, beware. Liaisons between humans and supernatural creatures nearly always end sadly.

This is seen in a Mi'kmaq story from eastern Canada retold by Dr Ruth Holmes Whitehead, in which a 'man of power' named Wsitiplaju asks Killer Whale Woman to marry him:

> 'Will you stay with me?' he asks.
>
> 'I will stay with you forever,' says Killer Whale Woman, 'if you can keep me away from the shore. You must take me into the forest. You must never again let me see the ocean. If you do this, *mu la'liwn wta'nuk, mu la'liwn sitmuk*[2] although it be for thirty years, so long I will be your wife . . .'

After many years of marriage, Wsitiplaju unwittingly makes camp beside the sea, lost in a fog. When morning comes and the fog clears, Killer Whale Woman sees the ocean. 'The sea

1 *The Destruction of Dá Derga's Hostel*, tr. Whitely Stokes, 1901.
2 Translation: 'If you don't take me to the ocean, if you don't take me to the shore'.

calls to her and she must answer it.' Taking her children with her, she plunges into the waves.

> Out to sea, swimming in the water, they see those three: those three Whales, leaping and spouting in the water, going away . . . Wsitiplaju screams. He cries out to them, 'Come back! My wife, come back to me. My son, bring your mother back! My little boys, come home to me.'
>
> His Killer Whale son turns in the water to look at him. '*Nu.* Father. *Telimïsk nkij, "mukk la'liew sitmuk".* My mother said to you, "You must not take me to the sea shore." You have not kept your word, and we are now going home.' . . . And the three Killer Whales moved off into the open sea.[3]

A strikingly similar tale is told in Ireland:

> A man who lived near Lough Sheelin, in County Meath, was annoyed by having his corn eaten night after night. So he sat up to watch; and to his astonishment a number of horses came up out of the lake, driven by a most beautiful woman, whom he seized and induced to marry him. She made the stipulation that she was never to be allowed to see the lake again; and for over twenty

3 Whitehead, Ruth Holmes, *Stories from the Six Worlds*, 42–3.

> years she lived happily with him, till one day she strolled out to look at the haymakers, and caught sight of the distant water. With a loud cry she flew straight to it, and vanished beneath the surface.[4]

There are conditions. There are always conditions. Even if the husband of a fairy bride wishes to keep his promises, he's bound to forget and break his word. In a story from the *Mahábhárata*, the goddess Ganga – the River Ganges herself – appears to King Shantanu as a beautiful woman. She agrees to marry him and they have seven children together, each of which she immediately drowns, having previously prohibited her husband from questioning any of her actions. When Shantanu begs her to spare the life of the eighth child, Ganga explains. All this was destined, springing from Brahma's curse on them both in a previous incarnation. Ganga's deeds were good, not evil: in drowning her children she has released them from the burden of mortal life. Since Shantanu has broken his promise, she must leave him – and, turning herself back into the river, she flows away.

In Marie de France's twelfth-century *lai*[5] the eponymous knight Lanval discovers a luxurious pavilion in the middle of a forest, home to a languorously beautiful fairy who gives him her love and showers him with rich gifts – so long as he promises never to speak of her. When he breaks his word, boasting that

---

4 Hartland, Edwin Sidney, *The Science of Fairy Tales*, 338.

5 The *Breton lai* is a short, rhymed tale of love or chivalry, often with a supernatural theme.

his beloved is more beautiful than Queen Guinevere, the fairy leaves him, returning only when he is condemned to die. She takes him away to Avalon – itself a realm of death.

Then there's the fairy Melusina, who married the Count of Lusignan on condition that he was never to see her on a Saturday. Of course the curious count spied on his bride and discovered with horror that 'the lovely form of Melusina ended below in a snake, gray and sky-blue, mixed with white'.[6] Melusina thereafter became a kind of banshee or death omen for the house of Lusignan.

In the Carmarthenshire story of *The Lady of Llyn y Fan Fach*, the Lady of the Lake gifts her mortal husband with wealth in the form of fairy sheep, swine and cattle, but warns that if he ever strikes her 'three causeless blows' she will leave him, never to return. Over the course of time, the lake lady's husband does strike her three times in reproof for her inhuman, fairy reactions – weeping at a christening and laughing at a funeral – and she departs, calling her cattle after her into the waters of the lake:

Mu wlfrech, moelfrech,
Brindled cow, bold freckled,
Mu olfrech, gwynfrech,
Spotted cow, white speckled,
Pedair cae tonn-frech,
Ye four field sward mottled,
Yr hen wynebwyn,
The old white-faced,

6 *The Fairy Mythology*, ed. Thomas Keightley, 482.

Ar las Geigen

And the grey Geigen

Gyda'r tarw gwyn

With the white bull

O lys y Brenin,

From the court of the King,

A'r llo du bach,

And thou little black calf,

Sydd ar y bach,

Suspended on the hook,

Dere dither, yb iach adre!

Come thou also, home again, home.

> . . . The little black calf, although it had been killed, came to life again, and descending from the hook, walked off with the rest of the cattle, sheep, goats, swine and horses at the command of the Lady of the Lake.[7]

The Lady of the Lake is desired not just for her beauty but also for the riches and good fortune she brings. A marriage is a political event, the collision and fusion of two families – sometimes of two different races – with all their separate histories, ambitions and expectations. The prohibitions and promises surrounding the union of a mortal with a fairy reflect the complexities and negotiations of real-life unions. Tales of fairy brides acknowledge and explore the difficulties of personal relations,

---

7 Thomas, W. Jenkyn, *The Welsh Fairy Book*, 6.

the balance of power between husband and wife, and the eternal Otherness of one's partner. They stress the importance of good faith, the remembering and keeping of promises. They warn that familiarity may breed contempt and that carelessness of a partner's wishes may lead to disaster. And some of them speak of years of silent resentment, of the apparently submissive bride who is only biding her time, looking for the first opportunity to desert her complacent partner.

David Thomson, in his collection of selkie legends, *The People of the Sea*, recounts the tale of a fisherman of North Uist who was out hunting cormorants on one of the skerries, or small islands.

> He found shelter for himself in a cleft o' the rocks and twas well after midnight when he looked down on the strand and he saw a number of people that were there, strangers to him, and they taking up, each of them, a skin from a heap of skins that was there. They put on the skins and in a moment they were changed into seals and they dived into the sea. And . . . he went to the place where the skins were and he saw one fine sealskin lying there and took and hid it under his coat . . . Well, he wasn't there long before a woman appeared before him.
>
> 'Give me,' said she, 'my clothing.'
>
> . . . 'Indeed,' said the man, 'I won't give it to you at all, but I shall bring you to my own home and you will be along with me,' he said.

> 'Oh,' she said, 'give me my clothes.'
>
> 'You'll not get them.' And he took off part of his own clothes, and put them on her.[8]

The selkie woman is forced to stay with the man and become his wife and bear his children. The tale makes clear that this is nothing better than rape. The fisherman not only compels the selkie to become his bride, he hides her sealskin so that she cannot shape-shift. She is a prisoner, and even when at last she discovers the hidden sealskin and returns to the sea, the fisherman thinks only of himself:

> 'It must have been that she saw me,' said he, 'when I was putting the skin into the heart of that stack of corn, and I am without a good woman tonight. Oh isn't it a pity that she got that skin for I was very happy when she was along with me.'[9]

I know people who find this story so disturbing they consider it unsuitable for children's ears, and I have sympathy with that point of view. It *is* disturbing, and it is meant to be. It's a cautionary tale and the moral isn't that the fisherman ought to have been more careful about where he hid that sealskin. The moral is that a forced marriage is no marriage at all.

The violence involved in catching and keeping a fairy bride (or any bride) against her will is made even clearer in the story

---

8 Thomas, David, *The People of the Sea*, 166.
9 Op. cit., 168.

of Wild Edric, told by the twelfth-century writer Walter Map in his lively and varied book of gossip, tales and reminiscences *De Nugis Curialium,* a title usually translated as 'Of Courtly Trifles', though a more colloquial rendering might be 'Courtly Bits and Pieces'.

Edric was a real person, Edricus Saluage, listed in Domesday Book as lord of the Shropshire manor of Ledbury North on the eve of the Norman Conquest. He was a charismatic war leader who held Shropshire for three years against William the Conqueror, and legends rapidly accumulated around his name. Writing only a hundred years or so later, Walter Map describes how, hunting in wild country with his page, Edric

> . . . came upon a large building at the edge of a forest . . . and when he was near it, seeing a light inside, he looked in and saw a great dance of noble ladies. They were most comely to look on, and finely clad in fair habits of linen only, and were greater and taller than our women. The knight remarked one among all the rest as excelling in face and form, desirable beyond any favourite of a king.[10]

Struck by love (or lust) Edric reacts with instant violence. He bursts in,

> . . . catches her by whom he has been caught, and

---

10 Map, Walter, *De Nugis Curialium*, 82.

> is instantly set upon by the rest; for a time he is delayed by a fierce struggle, but at last extricated by the utmost efforts of himself and his page, yet not quite undamaged – hurt in feet and legs by all that the nails and teeth of women could inflict. He took her with him, and for three days and nights used her as he would, yet could not wring a word from her.[11]

On the fourth day, the lady (in later legend named as Godda) speaks. She agrees to live with him and promises that his affairs will prosper until the day he reproaches her with her sisters or her origin. One day, returning from hunting, Edric calls his wife, and when she is slow to answer, exclaims angrily: '"Was it your sisters that kept you so long?"' But: 'The rest of his abuse was addressed to the air, for when her sisters were named she vanished.'

Today Edric is known as the leader of the local Wild Hunt, a death omen riding endlessly over the Shropshire hills. In *Shropshire Folklore* Charlotte Burne points out that 'Godda', the name of Edric's fairy bride, is close to that of Frau Gauden or Gode, the Wild Huntress of German tradition. And in a later reference to the story, Walter Map asserts that Godda 'vanished into air in open sight of many, because she took ill her husband's taunt that he had caught her from among the dead'.[12]

It is a mistake to regard the fairy bride as a passive, helpless

---

11 Op. cit., 83.
12 Op. cit., 191, 192.

victim. She may start out that way, in the selkie tales and other variants where a man steals a cloak – of fur, of feathers – to compel his bride to remain. But even in these stories, the selkie woman always returns to the sea, the man is always eventually abandoned, and often loses anything he has gained from the union, too. Thus the husband of the Lady of Llyn y Fan Fach loses all the goods she has brought as a dowry, and Wild Edric is left to ride the Shropshire hills – for all eternity – at the head of a frenzied rout. I don't see fairy brides as generic victims, but as part of a tradition of supernatural/human interchanges in which what is emphasised again and again is the danger, the instability of such liaisons, and the almost inevitable unhappiness and loss which will result. The difficulty can be seen to work the other way round, too. In a Danish ballad called *Agnete and the Merman*, a mortal maiden called Agnete accepts a Merman's proposal to join him under the sea and become his bride. She is mortal, he is fairy; she goes to him willingly, and it still doesn't work.

> They dwell together eight years and have seven sons. One day, Agnete, as she sits singing under the blue water, 'hears the clocks of England clang,' and straightway asks and receives permission to go on shore to church. She meets her mother at the church door. 'Where hast thou been these eight years, my daughter?' 'I have been at the bottom of the sea,' replies Agnete, 'and have seven sons by the Merman.' The Merman follows her into the church . . . 'Hearken, Agnete! Thy

> small bairns are crying for thee.' 'Let them cry as long as they will; – I shall not return to them."[13]

This is the story which inspired Matthew Arnold's classic poem *The Forsaken Merman*, in which the Merman's wife Margaret hears church bells ringing from the shore and fears she will 'lose my poor soul, Merman, here with thee'. Of course she too never comes back, since if she stays with the Merman she will lose her chance of heaven, her life-after-death.

Implicit in early medieval fairy tales is the belief that fairies are in a literal sense the dead. Wild Edric accuses his wife of coming 'from among the dead'. Melusina becomes a death omen, a banshee. Lanval's fairy appears at the point of his death to bear him away to Avalon. Even in the nineteenth-century story of the Lady of Llyn y Fan Fach, the fairy woman has the power to call her little black calf home, though it is dead and hanging on a hook. In the thirteenth-century romance *Sir Orfeo*, which transforms the Greek legend of Orpheus and Eurydice into a fairy tale, Orfeo dresses as a poor minstrel and sets out to find his wife Herodys who has been stolen away by the fairy king. Entering the underground fairy kingdom, he discovers it to be inhabited by those who have died violently or suddenly, in war, fire, or child-bed.

Fairyland is the land of death, and the dead are dangerous. If it's bad news to ravish a fairy, it's no better luck to be seduced by one. For every 'captured' fairy bride, there are plenty more who initiate the process themselves in an almost predatory

---

13 Buchanan, Robert, *Ballad Stories of the Affections*, vii.

way. Sex is clearly on the agenda in those sixteenth-century ballads which tell how the Queen of Fays abducts young men to be her lovers.

> Harp and carp, Thomas, she said,
> Harp and carp along wi' me
> And if ye dare to kiss my lips,
> Sure of your bodie I will be.[14]

For even when the mortal lovers of the fairy queen go willingly to their fate, there are still penalties to pay, and still the sense of visiting a dangerous Otherworld – neither earth, heaven nor hell.

> It was mirk, mirk night and there was nae stern
> light
> And they waded through red blude to the knee
> For a' the blude that's shed on earth
> Rins through the springs of that countrie.[15]

True Thomas kisses the Queen of Elfland and is enthralled to her for seven years: for seven years he must never speak a word; and finally she gives him the unwelcome gift of prophecy and 'a tongue that can never lie'. But Thomas might count himself lucky. Young Tam Lin, in the ballad of that name, has worse to fear:

---

14 'Thomas the Rhymer', *The Oxford Book of Ballads*, ed. James Kinsley, 8.

15 Op. cit., 10.

The queen o' Fairies she caught me,
In yon green hill to dwell,
And pleasant is the fairy-land;
But, an eerie tale to tell!

Ay at the end of seven years
We pay a tiend to hell;
I am sae fair and fu' of flesh
I'm fear'd it be mysel'.[16]

Only the courageous intervention of Janet, his mortal lover, saves him from damnation. The back door of fairyland leads down to hell.

The death aspect of fairy brides is not secondary to these stories, but essential. Fairy women come from the Otherworld, from the sea, from rivers and lakes, from the air – from places where living humans cannot go. They come, they touch mortal lives and wither them. In Russian legend, the spirits of dead, unmarried girls are called *rusalki*. They inhabit streams and woodlands and appear naked in the cold, or clothed only in thin white shifts. They inspired pity and fear:

> Peasant women would hang gifts of cloth, thread of a towel on the branches of trees for them. Yet they were also feared, for their loveless condition turned them into vengeful killers, who seduced

---

16 'Tam Lin', *The Oxford Book of Ballads*, ed. James Kinsley, 17.

> young men with their naked charms and the siren-like hypnotism of their songs, or by idly calling out men's names as they swung in the tree branches. The men who responded were lured into the water and drowned.[17]

Undines, mermaids, and other water and nature spirits share this dangerous character, which may be a lingering memory of Celtic goddesses such as Sulis at Bath and Sabrina of the Severn. Offerings were certainly made to rivers and springs in ancient times – and from the evidence of bog bodies, it's probable that human sacrifices were sometimes also made.

Perhaps the tale which points most directly to the death-bringing aspect of the fairy bride is that of ill-fated Völund and his brothers, who marry three swan-women they discover living in a valley ominously called Wolf-dale, by a lake named Wolf-water. *Völundrsaga* describes these swan-women as *Valkyriur* – Valkyries, Odin's maidens who ride over battles to choose the slain. Quite literally, death is their job: they are the original Northern Wild Hunt.

> Three times nine girls, but one girl rode ahead,
> white-skinned under her helmet;
> the horses were trembling, from their manes
> dew fell into the deep valleys,
> hail in the high woods;

17 Warner, Elizabeth, *Russian Myths*, 43.

> good fortune comes to men from there;
> all that I saw was hateful to me.[18]

In some traditions, those drops of dew are drops of blood.

In Japan you must beware of kitsune – supernatural foxes, who will love you to death.

> According to the fox-marriage legend, the fox in the guise of a pretty young woman will lead men into temptation to satisfy its desire. All the foxes will turn themselves into . . . fascinating women and exhaust the energy of their victims. The men victimized, it is believed, will die later.[19]

Kitsune share attributes of the trickster, as Lafcadio Hearn explains:

> Goblin foxes are peculiarly dreaded in Izumo for three evil habits attributed to them. The first is that of deceiving people by enchantment, whether for revenge or pure mischief. The second is that of quartering themselves as retainers upon some family and thereby making that family a terror to the neighbours. The third and worst is

---

18 *The Poetic Edda*, tr. Carolyne Larrington, Oxford 1999, 128.
19 Nozaki, Kiyoshi, *Kitsuné: Japan's Fox of Mystery, Romance and Humor*, 26.

> that of entering into people and taking diabolical possession of them.[20]

Their tendency to seduce men is well attested. A young man named Yasutaka meets a woman in the pine groves by moonlight. 'She seemed shy, covering her face with a pictured fan. She looked pretty, with stray tresses of the side-locks playing on her forehead and cheeks.' At first Yasutaka flirts with the young woman, but gradually he becomes suspicious. Remembering rumours of a fox spirit haunting the area, he draws his sword and threatens to cut her throat – upon which, leaving behind a noxious smell, 'the fascinating girl changed herself into a fox and took flight'.[21]

Yasutaka was wise. Even when both parties are content to live together, something will occur to divide them, as in the Japanese story of the Crane Wife, who comes in woman's form to her weaver husband in gratitude for having been rescued, in bird form, from a trap. She weaves beautiful brocades for him, but gradually becomes more and more pale and ill. When he discovers her plucking out her own feathers to incorporate into the cloth, she vanishes for ever.

Whether mortals woo, ravish or capture supernatural women, whether mortals themselves are carried off or seduced, marrying a fairy bride nearly always leads to grief at best, to death at worst. The Great Silkie of Sule Skerry marries an earthly woman, and fathers her child, but appears at her bed foot, 'a grumly guest',

---

20 Hearn, Lafcadio, *Glimpses of Unfamiliar Japan*, 302.
21 Nozaki, Kiyoshi, *Kitsuné: Japan's Fox of Mystery, Romance and Humor*, 51–3.

to predict the death of himself and his half-human son. Perhaps most sinister of all is the Irish Love Talker, or Gancanagh:

> I met the Love-talker one eve in the glen
> He was handsomer than any of our handsome young men,
> His eyes were blacker than the sloe, his voice sweeter far
> Than the crooning of old Kevin's pipes beyond in Coolnagar.
>
> I was bound for the milking with a heart fair and free –
> My grief! my grief! that bitter hour drained the life from me;
> I thought him human lover, though his lips on mine were cold,
> And the breath of death blew keen on me within his hold.[22]

For: 'Who meets the Love-talker must weave her shroud soon.'

No: the next time you meet a lady 'full beautiful, a faery's child', wandering suggestively in the meadows or swimming, white as flowers of the foam, in ocean or lake, don't follow her into her elfin grot. Stop your ears! Take to your heels! Or risk wandering alone and deserted on the cold hill side, haggard and woebegone, and quite possibly dead.

---

22 Carbery, Ethna, *The Love Talker*, from *The Fourwinds of Eirrin*, 18.

After the wedding

After the wedding
the prince and the goosegirl
rode off to spend their lives in a hall of mirrors.

After the wedding
roses sprang from the grave and twined their way
right up the church, to the very top of the steeple.

After the wedding
little white doves flew down,
and pecked out the eyes of the two jealous sisters.

After the wedding
the soldier shouldered his musket
and returned to the wars.

After the wedding
the orphan child limped home in paper shoes
over a pavement clinking with broken glass.

Enchanted objects

Why do fairy tales contain so many mundane enchanted objects? Humble things like boots, purses, pots and kettles, tables, geese and donkeys? Wish-fulfilment is one answer. Not everyone wants to be a hero, and magical crowns, swords or rings are unlikely to be much use to ordinary folk. Most of the time what most people really want is labour-saving devices – things that will help in everyday life, rest their aching feet or fill their empty bellies.

In Joseph Jacobs' tale *The Three Soldiers*, a sergeant, a corporal and a private returning from the wars allow an old woman to share their fire for three consecutive nights. On the first night, she gives the sergeant an old purse.

> 'Oh thank you, marm,' said the sergeant, 'but I wouldn't deprive you of it, especially as there is nothing in it.'
>
> 'That may be so now,' said the old woman, 'but take it in your hand and turn it upside down, and,

> while you hold it like that, gold pieces will come pouring out of it.'[1]

It's significant that the magic purse doesn't *look* anything special. Far from bulging with money, it seems empty: the gold only appears if the owner turns it upside down and shakes it – the action of a poor man who hopes against hope that some small coin may have been overlooked inside. Small expectations, amply rewarded.

On the second night, the old woman presents the corporal with a tablecloth:

> Said he, 'Thank you, marm, kindly, but we soldiers rarely use tablecloths when we are eating our vittles.'
>
> 'Yes, but this gives you vittles to eat,' said the old woman. 'Whenever you put this on a table or on the ground and call out, "Be covered!" the finest dinner you could eat at once comes upon it.'

The glint of humour – 'We soldiers rarely use tablecloths' – nevertheless calls attention to the rough poverty of the soldier's life. A genteel item like an ordinary tablecloth is the last thing he is likely to need, but a magic one that provides 'vittles' is welcome indeed.

On the final night, the old woman hands a whistle to the private soldier.

---

1 Jacobs, Joseph, 'The Three Soldiers', *Europa's Fairy Book*, 72 et seq.

> 'And what's this for?' said the private. 'I can't play on the whistle.'
>
> 'But you can blow it,' said she, 'and whenever you blow it out will come a regiment of armed men that will do whatever you tell them.'

Possessed of such a gift, the unskilled, insignificant private soldier becomes as powerful as a general. This tale is aimed at poor folk, who will understand it better than the well-off. It magnifies tiny, basic pleasures – the delight of discovering a five-pound note in an old coat pocket, the offer of a good square meal when you're hungry, the security of having comrades at your back. Money, food and safety: we take them for granted, but for those who don't possess them, they loom large.

If it takes cold, weary hours to trudge to the nearest town, what more natural than to wish for boots which could carry you leagues in a single stride? If all you have for protection is a cudgel, what a comfort if that cudgel were a magic one, which could beat your enemies into submission while you stood safely at a distance! When times are hard, when food is scarce, what better than a little table

> which was not particularly beautiful, and was made of common wood, but which had one good property; if anyone set it out and said: 'Little table, spread yourself,' the good little table was at once covered with a clean little cloth, and a plate was there, and a knife and fork beside it, and dishes with boiled meats and roasted meats . . . and a

> great glass of red wine which shone to make the heart glad.[2]

I love that the table isn't 'particularly beautiful'. It doesn't need to be. If you're hungry, who cares what the thing looks like? What's important is that it provides. (And it clears itself afterwards, so there's no need to wash the dishes.)

Even this bourgeois dream of meat and wine, a place-setting and a tablecloth was beyond imagination for some folk. In the following story I am moved not only by the poverty of the characters, but by the simplicity of their wish-fulfilment. It takes so little to make them happy.

> There was a poor but good little girl who lived alone with her mother, and they no longer had anything to eat. So the child went into the forest, and there an aged woman met her who was aware of her sorrow, and presented her with a little pot, which when she said: 'Cook, little pot, cook,' would cook good, sweet porridge, and when she said, 'Stop, little pot,' it ceased to cook. The girl took the pot home to her mother, and now they were freed from their poverty and hunger, and ate sweet porridge as often as they chose.
>
> Once on a time when the girl had gone out, her mother said, 'Cook, little pot, cook.' And it

---

2 'The Wishing Table, the Gold-Ass, and the Cudgel in the Sack', KHM 36, *Grimm's Fairy Tales*, 177

> did cook and she ate till she was satisfied, and then she wanted to stop the pot cooking, but did not know the word. So it went on cooking and the porridge rose over the edge, and still it cooked on until the kitchen and whole house were full, and then the next house, and then the whole street, just as if it wanted to satisfy the hunger of the whole world, and there was the greatest distress, but no one knew how to stop it. At last when only one single house remained, the child came home and said, 'Stop, little pot,' and it stopped and gave up cooking, and whoever wished to return to the town had to eat his way back.[3]

Despite the comic ending – the town buried in porridge like another Pompeii – the significantly tragic line 'as if it wanted to satisfy the hunger of the whole world' undercuts the fun. *The hunger of the whole world* is a big thing to acknowledge in such a little fairy tale.

Wish-fulfilment is not to be scorned. Someone, at some time, said, 'How cold it is! I wish we could tame fire! If only we could have a little one burning all the time, to cook our food and keep us warm!' Someone else said, 'Grinding grain is weary work. Do you see how strongly the wind blows and the river rushes? What if we could harness their power to turn our millstones?' Much more recently, someone said, 'What if we could make a horseless carriage?' And we're still at it.

---

3 'Sweet Porridge', KHM 103, *Grimm's Fairy Tales*, 475.

Driverless cars . . . self-cleaning glass . . . solar panels sitting on the roof . . . The what-ifs of this world, prompted mainly by discomfort and the desire for an easier life, have been the mainspring of human invention. And invention is the stuff of fairy tales.

But there's more to it than wish-fulfilment. These stories aren't naïve. They're intended to amuse, and much of their success is due to the deliberate manipulation of incongruities. The Gold-Ass in the story of the Wishing Table spews golden coins out of its mouth – and shits them out of its backside. Aladdin's powerful djinn is shut up not in a golden casket, but in a common earthenware lamp. In a Japanese tale, *The Magic Kettle*, retold by Andrew Lang, a poor man finds a dirty old kettle which is inhabited by a spirit-animal, a tanuki or raccoon-dog. In fact the kettle *is* the tanuki, the tanuki *is* the kettle – but for practical purposes it is useless. Each time the old man uses it to try and boil water, it transforms and leaps around the room chasing its tail and wreaking havoc. At last the old man sells it to a friend who has the sense to recognise that what he has bought is not a utensil, but a creature. He asks the tanuki's permission to put it on show, and crowds come to watch it transform:

> In an instant the handle began to change into a head and the spout into a tail, while the four paws appeared at the sides. 'Dance,' said Jimmu, and the tanuki did his steps, and moved first on one side and then on the other, till the people could not stand it any longer and began to dance

> too. Gracefully he led the fan dance, and glided without a pause into the shadow dance and the umbrella dance, and it seemed as if he might go on dancing for ever.[4]

The tanuki-kettle may be no good for boiling water, but it makes its new, more imaginative owner rich, and the story's sense of fun and wonder is well expressed by the Japanese title, *Bunbuku Chagama*, which apparently translates as 'happiness bubbling over like a teapot'.

We grow accustomed to the magic of ordinary household things. (The electric kettle sitting on your kitchen counter *is* enchanted, you know. You couldn't boil the water by yourself.) But the stories warn us to treat magical objects with respect. Used moderately and with wisdom, they can help us get on in life. But use them carelessly or greedily, and disaster will follow. Think what happened to the Sorcerer's Apprentice! Read the instructions, remember the magic words – or the porridge pot will overflow, the enchanted salt-mill will go on grinding and grinding until the entire sea is salt. Avoid fossil fuels – save electricity! Don't kill the goose which lays the golden eggs.

Most stories of the 'magic tablecloth, magic purse, magic cudgel' variety[5] develop in a fairly standard way. Three poor fellows, soldiers, tailors, carpenters and the like, are lucky enough to be presented with three magical gifts. The first two men are then tricked out of their possessions – in *The Wishing Table*, by

---

4 Lang, Andrew, 'The Magic Kettle', *The Crimson Fairy Book.*
5 Aarne-Thompson tale type 563: Three Magic Gifts.

a dastardly innkeeper; in *The Three Soldiers*, by an unscrupulous princess – but the third, whose prize is usually a magic cudgel, is able to turn the tables on the villain and regain the treasures. The three then live happily for the rest of their lives. A story called *The Knapsack, the Hat and the Horn*,[6] however, pursues to its logical extreme the consequences of owning a magical object when the owner's greed is uncontrolled. It isn't a happy tale.

Three poor brothers set out together to seek their fortunes. Coming to mountains covered in silver and in gold, the first two brothers fill their pockets and head for home. However the youngest brother is not yet content and journeys on until, hungry and lost, he comes upon a table under a tree, spread with a cloth and covered with a hot meal, 'the steam of which rose up to meet him'. He sits and eats, and when he has finished he folds up the tablecloth and takes it with him.

So far, so good: an everlasting supply of food is better than silver or gold: the boy has chosen better than his brothers and you might suppose that like the young man who obtained the Wishing Table he might exclaim to himself, 'With this, you have enough for your whole life.'[7] Not so, and now the story begins to darken. He comes to the hut of a charcoal burner who offers him shelter and a share of his meagre supper: 'One day is like another, and every night potatoes!' Of course the hero shakes out his tablecloth and a wonderful meal appears. The

6 'The Knapsack, the Hat and the Horn', KHM 54, *Grimm's Fairy Tales*, 258.

7 'The Wishing Table, the Gold-Ass, and the Cudgel in the Sack', KHM 36, *Grimm's Fairy Tales*, 180.

charcoal burner is amazed but honest. He wants the tablecloth, but he doesn't steal it. He offers a swap.

> 'Listen, your tablecloth has my approval; it would be a fine thing for me in this forest, where no one ever cooks me anything good. I will propose an exchange to you; there in the corner hangs a soldier's knapsack, which is certainly old and shabby, but in it lie concealed wonderful powers . . . every time you tap it with your hand, a corporal comes out with six men armed from head to foot, and they do whatsoever you command them.'[8]

The charcoal burner is willing to part with the magic knapsack because although he knows it's an object with *intrinsic* value, it's not actually valuable to *him*. He never uses it. What need has a charcoal burner of armed men? The hero seizes the opportunity. He agrees to the exchange. The next day, once he has gone a little distance into the wood, he taps the knapsack. Out come the soldiers. He orders them to march straight back to the charcoal burner's hut and retrieve the tablecloth.

What is happening? Instead of the naïve, good-natured hero we expect, here is the con-man himself – ruthless and calculating. Over the next two days he tricks two more innocent charcoal burners in exactly the same way. From one of them he

---

8 'The Knapsack, the Hat and the Horn', KHM 54, *Grimm's Fairy Tales*, 260.

takes a hat which, when turned around on the head, causes volleys of cannon to fire, and from the other he takes a horn which, if blown, destroys walls and lays villages and towns in ruin.

By now, this so-called hero has surely lost any sympathy we might once have felt for him. He could have been content with silver or with gold, or with an endless supply of free meals. But it turns out that what he wants is power, and the knapsack is full of it, and what use to leave it hanging in the corner? His success depends on his ability to recognise a very nasty truth: if you have power and are ruthless enough, you can have everything else you want, too.

Possessed of all these magical objects he heads home to find his rich brothers living in a fine house. When they see his ragged coat, shabby hat and worn-out knapsack they make fun of him and drive him out. In a rage he taps the knapsack till a hundred and fifty men are beating up his brothers. Civil disturbance breaks out as the neighbours pile in, trying to help. The King sends an army to restore peace, but the invincible hero turns his hat. Cannons fire, the King's men are routed, and the boy demands the hand of the princess in marriage.

Unsurprisingly, the princess – 'the false wife' as she is rather unfairly termed – is unhappy about being forcibly married to a violent stranger,[9] so with sweet talk she persuades her new

---

9 Oddly, the Grimms feel compelled to come up with disapproving explanations for her dislike of him. In Jack Zipes' translation of the 1812 version of the story it's because her new husband is 'an old guy'; in the 1857 version translated by Margaret Hunt it's because he is 'a common man who wore a shabby hat.' It's as if the mere fact of marriage, for them, trumped everything.

husband to reveal the source of his power, seizes the knapsack herself and orders the soldiers to drive him out. Our hero still has the hat – but the princess inveigles that away from him too. Now all he has left is his horn. Will he use it? Yes he will. In the final, 1857 edition of the tale:

> [In] great anger he blew it with all his strength. Instantly all walls, fortifications, towns and villages, toppled down and crushed the King and his daughter to death. And had he not put down the horn and had blown just a little longer, everything would have been in ruins, and not one stone would have been left standing on another. Then no one opposed him any longer, and he made himself King of the whole country.

Bleak as this ending is, a Pyrrhic victory emptied of love, friendship or any possibility of human relationships, the ending of the original 1812 edition of the story is bleaker still.

> So he blew it, and the villages, cities, and all the fortresses collapsed instantly into heaps of rubble. Then he alone was king and blew his horn until he died.[10]

Did Wilhelm Grimm tone down this earlier ending because

10 'The Tablecloth, the Knapsack, the Cannon Hat, and the Horn', *The Original Folk and Fairy Tales of the Brothers Grimm*, 129.

he found it too nihilistic? Perhaps, but I think he was wrong. Both endings are indeed very dark, but to leave the hero as King, even over a desolate land, is to render the story pointless. Whoever told this tale for the first time knew what they were doing. He who wanted everything ends up with nothing, and the trajectory of this increasingly greedy, power-hungry protagonist rightly ends in self-destruction.

Hardworking girls: the role of fairy-tale heroines

Heroines, you will note, not 'fairy-tale princesses'. For although there are many princesses in fairy tales, the heroine herself is just as often a peasant, a servant girl, a woodcutter's daughter or even, like the unnamed heroine of *Sweetheart Roland*, the child of a magic-worker, magician or witch. Sleeping Beauty and Snow-White are princesses born, yes, but Cinderella and Beauty are merchant's daughters, Rapunzel a peasant woman's child, the girl in Rumpelstiltskin a miller's daughter, and so on. Many are true heroines, active and adventurous, like Maid Maleen whose magic powers save herself and her lover from a giant, or the girl in *Fitcher's Bird* who rescues herself and her sisters and brings about the death of a wizard. Yet the popular notion of a fairy-tale heroine is that of a Barbie-blonde princess dressed in pink silk and diamonds, lying on a bed in a tower, awaiting rescue from a prince on a white horse – and therefore a terrible role model for little girls. Why should this be?

I don't happen to believe that the purpose either of literature in general or of fairy tales in particular is, in fact, to provide role models, but even if it were, fairy tales are more even-handed in their treatment of the sexes than they are usually given credit for. Nor are they exclusively or even generally concerned with princes and princesses, magic and marriages. Of the two hundred and ten stories in the collected edition of Grimm's *Children's and Household Tales*, almost half are tales about animals (*The Bremen Town Musicians*), household objects (*The Straw, the Coal and the Bean*), simpletons (*Frederick and Catherine*); they are morality tales (*The Fisherman and his Wife*), cautionary tales (*Frau Trude*), nonsense tales (*Fair Katrinelje and Pif-Paf-Poultrie*), saints' tales, tales about Death, the Devil, God and St Peter, and pious fables (*Our Lady's Little Glass*).[1] Of the remaining hundred or so which correspond more closely to what we're used to thinking a 'fairy tale' should be, at least fifty contain main or prominent female characters, over thirty of whom rescue brothers or sweethearts, save themselves or others and achieve wealth and happiness. It's not a bad ratio.

Fairy tales approve and reward the virtues of innocence, industry and good nature in both female and male protagonists. Innocence in male characters is often marked by a boy's apparent stupidity or folly, like Dummling in *The Golden Goose*. In female characters it can be indicated by extreme youth: for instance Snow-White is a child of seven when her stepmother drives her out, and in the following quotation from *The Seven Ravens*, the heroine is interchangeably referred to as 'the maiden' or 'the child':

1 All of these tales are in Grimm.

> The maiden went forth into the wide world to search for her brothers and set them free, cost what it might. And now she went onwards, far, far, to the very end of the world. Then she came to the sun, but it was too hot and terrible, and devoured little children. Hastily she ran away, and ran to the moon, but it was far too cold, and also awful and malicious, and when it saw the child it said, 'I smell, I smell the flesh of men.' . . . So the maiden went onwards until she came to the Glass Mountain . . .[2]

The maiden finally rescues her brothers (transformed at her birth into ravens by their father's curse) by cutting off one of her own fingers and using it as a key to unlock the door of the Glass Mountain. In this tale, as in its better-known analogue *The Six Swans*, the sister's faithful exertions restore her brothers to their human shape. (The tale never tells if she got her finger back.) There are plenty of other fairy stories about the bond between siblings, and more often than not it is the girl who saves the day. As Alison Lurie has pointed out in *Don't Tell The Grown-Ups*,[3] it is Gretel, not Hansel, who pushes the witch into the oven. Or there's Mollie Whuppie,[4] abandoned in the woods by her parents, whose quick wits defeat a giant and win the hand of three princes in marriage for her and her two sisters.

---

2 'The Seven Ravens', KHM 25, *Grimm's Fairy Tales*, 137.
3 Lurie, Alison, *Don't Tell The Grown-Ups*, 18.
4 Jacobs, Joseph, *English Fairy Tales*.

Or the Orkney tale of Kate Crackernuts,[5] who, when her own mother conjures a sheep's head on to her prettier stepsister's shoulders, wraps 'a fine linen cloth' around her sister's head 'and took her by the hand and they both went out to seek their fortune'. Coming to a king's castle 'who had two sons, and one of them was sickening away to death, and no one could find out what ailed him', Kate offers her services, following the prince at midnight into a green hill where he dances all night with the fairies until he drops from exhaustion. By persistence, courage, and intelligence, Kate cures both the prince and her sister, and: 'The sick son married the well sister and the well son married the sick sister, and they all lived and died happy and never drank out of a dry cappy.'

Fairy-tale heroines to me do not signify passivity and helplessness. Far more often they exhibit resourcefulness, resilience, courage. In the Norwegian fairy tale *The Master-Maid*,[6] the prince would be eaten by the troll to whom he has pledged his work, were it not for the wisdom and magical power of the eponymous Master-Maid who lives in the troll's house. The prince succeeds in each perilous task only by following the Master-Maid's advice. Finally the troll orders the Master-Maid to kill the prince and cook him. Instead she cuts his little finger and lets three drops of blood fall. As the troll sleeps, she escapes with the prince and a great deal of magical treasure; when the troll awakes to demand if the meal is cooked, the drops of blood answer for her: 'Not yet'; 'Nearly'; and, 'It is

---

5 Briggs, Katherine, *Dictionary of British Folk-Tales*, Part A, Vol 1, 344.

6 Dasent, Sir George, *Popular Tales from the Norse*, 137.

boiled dry.' The troll pursues the couple, but the Master-Maid flings magical impediments in his path. Prince and Master-Maid are finally married, but not before a further development in which the prince forgets her, and is rescued on the verge of marrying the wrong woman . . .

In one of my favourite English fairy tales *Mr Fox*,[7] the heroine Lady Mary may initially be deceived by the sly flattery of her suitor, but she is inquisitive and brave as well as rich and beautiful. She discovers for herself the bloody secrets of Mr Fox's castle, and turns the tables on her would-be murderer in the neatest and most self-possessed of ways. The story quite definitely approves female curiosity and courage: without these qualities, the heroine would have joined the list of this serial killer's victims. There is no marriage at all at the end of the story, and one feels Lady Mary will give the next suitor a very hard look indeed.

In the story variously known as *Donkeyskin*, *Allerleirauh*, or *Cap o' Rushes* the heroine flees her father's house to save herself from an incestuous marriage:

> When the king's daughter saw there was no hope of turning her father's heart, she resolved to run away. In the night when everyone was asleep, she got up and took three different things from her treasures, a golden ring, a golden spinning wheel, and a golden reel. The three dresses of sun, moon and stars she placed into a nutshell, put on her

---

7 Jacobs, Joseph, *English Fairy Tales*, 148.

> mantle of all kinds of fur, and blackened her face and hands with soot. Then she commended herself to God and went away.[8]

Disguised in extraordinary clothes, a donkey skin, a coat made of all kinds of different furs, or a cloak made of rushes, she sets out for another kingdom and finds rough work in the palace kitchens. On seeing the prince or heir of the house, she obtains his attention by a series of tricks (mysterious appearances at dances; golden rings dropped in wine cups) and finally marries him. You might call it enterprising.

Many are the heroines who get the better of the Devil himself – in fact, this dark gentleman rarely fares well in folktales. Remember the farmer who sells his soul in return for twenty years of good harvests? And when the time comes to pay up, his clever wife saves him. 'My man won't be a minute, sir, he's just getting his things together, and please take a mouthful to eat while you wait!' she calls to the Devil, handing him a pie into which she has baked a red-hot griddle. When he bites into it, burning his tongue and breaking his teeth, she interrupts his howls with the merry cry, 'And I'm coming too, to cook for you both!' – at which the terrified Devil takes to his heels.[9] Of course it's comical: but note that the farmer's wife employs her wits and skills, and defeats the Devil, in a particularly feminine way.

Just as wives can be cleverer than husbands, daughters are

8 'Allerleirauh', KHM 65, *Grimm's Fairy Tales*, 322.

9 I have been telling this story for years but am currently unable to trace it.

frequently wiser than their fathers. In one of the Grimms' tales, a peasant digging a field discovers treasure – and ignores his daughter's advice:

> When they had dug nearly the whole of the field, they found in the earth a mortar made of pure gold. 'Listen,' said the father to the girl, 'as our lord the King has graciously given us this field, we ought to give him this mortar in return for it.' 'Father,' said the daughter, 'if we have the mortar without having the pestle as well, we shall have to get the pestle, so you had much better say nothing about it.' But he would not obey her, and carried the mortar to the king . . .[10]

It's a bad decision. Sure enough, the greedy king wants the pestle too, and imprisons the peasant for failing to produce it. The daughter's wit and courage saves her father and wins marriage with the king – whom she later kidnaps in order to teach him a much-needed lesson.

Heroines such as these know their own minds and make their own decisions. They are prudent, determined, wily and brave. They are so far from the stereotype of the fairy-tale princess that one has to ask how it arose. If there are so many stories with strong heroines, why are they not more widely known?

Traditional tales change subtly each time they are told as,

10 'The Peasant's Wise Daughter', KHM 94, *Grimm's Fairy Tales*, 437.

consciously or unconsciously, the teller adjusts and tinkers with them to appeal to the taste of the moment's audience. We cannot say that this or that version of any traditional story is 'original'. All we can do is look, every time, at who is telling it, and to whom, and for what purpose. 'The prominence of certain stories is in itself symptomatic of cultural production – of the way in which culture constitutes itself by constituting us.'[11] Despite the title, the first two volumes of Wilhelm and Jacob Grimm's *Children's and Household Tales* (1812 and 1815) were intended for adults and scholars. When in 1825 the brothers decided to bring out 'a smaller edition of 50 tales . . . geared to the tastes of bourgeois families'[12] and likely to be read to or by children, they rewrote or omitted many stories with sexual content, yet included some we would today consider inappropriately violent. Each successive generation uses, interprets and censors fairy tales according to its own standards. Not intrinsic excellence, but an ongoing process of social and editorial bias towards passive, gentle heroines has favoured and raised to prominence those tales we recognise as 'classic', including four of the best-known of all: *Sleeping Beauty*, *Snow-White*, *Cinderella*, and *Beauty and the Beast*.

Even these heroines turn out on closer scrutiny to be less passive than you might suppose. (It's true that the Sleeping Beauty hasn't much to do except await true love's kiss, but then the prince hasn't much to do either: as I argue elsewhere,

11 Tatar, Maria, *Off With Their Heads!*, 230.

12 Zipes, Jack, ed: *The Oxford Companion to Fairy Tales*, OUP 2015, 246.

this is a story about time, not about people.) Abandoned in the forest, little Snow-White doesn't lie down and die like the Babes in the Wood. She keeps going till she finds the house of the seven dwarfs, where she pays her way by working:

> The dwarfs said, 'Will you attend to our housekeeping for us? Cook, make beds, wash, sew and knit? If you like to do all this for us, and keep everything in order for us, you may stay and shall want for nothing.'
>
> 'With all my heart,' said the child. So she stayed, keeping everything in excellent order. The dwarfs went every day to the mountains, to find copper and gold, and came home in the evening, and then their supper had to be ready.[13]

I see nothing wrong with this bargain. Both sides get something out of it, both are satisfied.

Cinderella, too, works hard 'from morning till night'; not voluntarily but forced to do so by her stepmother and stepsisters. But how she reacts – passive and resigned, or actively engaged – depends upon which of the two best-known versions you read. Even as a child I was aware of this. In my big picture-book I could study full-colour illustrations of the fairy godmother, the pumpkin coach and the glass slipper – derived from Perrault's *Cendrillon*. But the old-fashioned, closely printed book of fairy

---

13 'Little Snow-White', KHM 53, *Grimm's Fairy Tales*, 249.

tales handed down from my mother told instead of a magical tree and helpful doves. I preferred this, the version collected by the brothers Grimm; and I now see why.

The difference between the two versions is striking. Although Perrault's tale predates the Grimms' by over a century, it has been remodelled to amuse a sophisticated salon audience – it's one of "those tight-laced, high-heeled tales of 'the tea-cup times'" as Sir George Dasent[14] describes them. Perrault's Cinderella is long-suffering, patient and gentle, while the fairy godmother is a civilised figure, a mother-substitute who launches her protégé into society with the élan of a wealthy patron. The magical transformations of pumpkin, mice, rats and lizards are delightful conjuring tricks. At the end, Cinderella demonstrates her gentility by forgiving her stepsisters and marrying them to 'two great lords of the court'. It is all in excellent taste.

Tastes change, however, and by the time the Grimm brothers were beginning to collect folk and fairy stories in the first decade of the nineteenth century, the Romantic movement was welcoming a wilder, more spontaneous type of tale. The heroine of *Aschenputtel* (most English translations rename her Cinderella) has agency; her story is rougher, less literary, more magical, savage in tone and detail. There is blood within the shoe; the dead return as birds . . . In a motif similar to that of *Beauty and the Beast*, the girl asks her father to bring her not beautiful clothes, pearls and jewels – as her stepsisters do – but 'the first branch which knocks against your hat on the

---

14 Dasent, Sir George, *Popular Tales from the Norse*, I.

way home'. Planting the hazel twig on her mother's grave, she waters it with her tears, and:

> [A] little white bird always came on the tree, and if Cinderella expressed a wish, the bird threw down to her what she had wished for.[15]

In contrast to the civilised patronage of Perrault's fairy godmother, the power this Cinderella derives from her dead mother's grave is a miraculous inheritance: life rising from the grave in green sap and leaves, the white soul fluttering in the branches.

Cinderella calls down all the birds of the air to perform the impossible task of picking out peas and lentils from the ashes, and once the stepmother and sisters have sped away to the festival, she goes to her mother's grave and calls,

> 'Shiver and quiver, little tree,
> Silver and gold throw down on me.'
> Then the bird threw a gold and silver dress down to her, and slippers embroidered with silk and silver.

Cinderella stage-manages the entire affair for the next three nights: no panic, no deadlines, no clocks striking twelve.

> When evening came she wished to leave, and

15 'Cinderella', KHM 21, Grimm's Fairy Tales, 128 et seq.

> the King's son followed her and wanted to see into which house she went. But she sprang away from him and into the garden behind the house. There stood a beautiful pear tree . . . She clambered so nimbly between the branches that the King's son did not know where she had gone. He waited until her father came and said to him, 'The unknown maiden has escaped from me and I believe she has climbed up the pear-tree.' The father thought, 'Can it be Cinderella?' and had an axe brought, and cut the tree down, but no one was in it. And when they got into the kitchen, Cinderella lay there among the ashes, for she had jumped down on the other side of the tree, had taken the beautiful dress to the bird on the hazel tree, and put on her old grey gown.

'When evening came, she wished to leave': here is a girl with her own mind and her own agenda. She runs, climbs trees, jumps out of them, performs lightning costume-changes, and lies low to deceive the family. *Cinderella* is regarded as the archetypical 'rags-to-riches' story, but a girl who can obtain whatever she wishes from a magical hazel tree is not poor, and to me it seems that a great part of the pleasure the story affords is that of revenge. The Grimms' Cinderella gets her own back on everyone who has ill-treated her. Her neglectful father loses his pigeon house and pear tree (chopped to pieces); her ambitious stepsisters slice off their toes and heels, filling the golden shoe with blood, and finally (while squeamish modern readers wince) pigeons peck out both their eyes. I preferred and still prefer the Grimms' version to that of Perrault. Yet it is Perrault's version most children know, the one adapted by Walt Disney, the one most often found in picture books. Adult gatekeepers – parents, editors, publishers – have chosen the docile charm of Perrault's Cinderella as a more suitable example for children (of tractability and good manners) rather than the energy, wild magic and vengeance of the Grimms'.

When her father loses all his money, Beauty of *Beauty and the Beast* rolls up her sleeves and gets to work: in Madame de Beaumont's classic eighteenth-century text:

> Beauty rose at four in the morning and made haste to have the house clean, and dinner ready for the family. In the beginning she found it very difficult, for she had not been used to work as a servant, but in less than two months she grew stronger and healthier than ever.[16]

Beauty bravely insists on saving her father's life by going to live with the Beast, but she has moral as well as physical courage: when the Beast asks, as he constantly does, 'Beauty, will you be my wife?' she refuses, because even though she grows more and more fond of him, *she is not ready to say yes.* Why aren't we all cheering? Freudian interpretations suggest this and other stories of monster or animal bridegrooms are all

---

16 Opie, Iona and Peter, 'Beauty and the Beast', *The Classic Fairy Tales*, 182.

about the awakening of sexuality: the young girl fears brutish male sexuality before coming to womanhood and embracing it. But Madame de Beaumont's Beast treats Beauty from the beginning with melancholy civility, and she loses any fear of him months before the end of the story. If *Beauty and the Beast* is a parable about sex, it's less about overcoming fear than it is about withstanding social pressure and taking the time to know your own mind. Finally – she leaves it rather late, but that's narrative tension for you – Beauty recognises the ugly but courteous Beast as someone she genuinely loves. On her promise to marry him, the spell is broken. Beauty has rescued him, and the Beast is restored to his true shape – which is of course that of a handsome prince.

Is there any real danger that a little girl – this sort of worry is always about girls – might read these tales and come away with the idea that you can loll around wearing pink satin till a man comes to marry you? (The same disapproval and disquiet is never levelled at the many male characters in fairy stories who marry princesses.) Fairy tales are not Mills and Boon romances: they do not offer romance: they cannot be read that way. They tell us to be active, to use our wits, to be undaunted, to see what we want and to go for it. Marriage-with-the-prince-or-princess is a metaphor for success in life. How else can the stories convey it? *The Brave Little Tailor*, the soldier in *The Blue Light*, the soldier in *The Twelve Dancing Princesses*, the boy with the Golden Goose – no one seems to have any trouble recognising, in their tales, a royal marriage as a symbol of personal happiness and well-earned worldly success.

The lost kings of Fairyland

Who reigns in faeryland? Many modern fantasies concern themselves with the fate of a doomed but brilliant young man in thrall to a beautiful, capricious and often cruel faerie queen. Often it's the heroine's role to try and rescue the young man, who would be her own boyfriend or lover if only he were free. The theme has its proximate source in two ballads, *Tam Lin* and *Thomas the Rhymer* – especially the former: Janet saves her lover Tam Lin from the worst possible fate (hellfire) by her bravery and single-mindedness. She goes to Miles Cross at midnight and waits for the Fairy Rade – the fairy cavalcade – to pass by, pulls Tam Lin from his white horse and holds on to him while he is transformed into a number of horrifying shapes. Finally he appears in his own shape, a naked man: Janet casts her cloak around him and claims him as her true love, while the furious fairy queen can only threaten and rage.

In the last fifty years there have been scores of retellings of this tale – picture-books, short stories and novels.[1] *Tam Lin* is

1 The most distinguished include Alan Garner's *Red Shift*, Diana

popular because we want strong women and it offers us two: staunch Janet and the powerful Queen of Fays. The traditional motif of the tithe to hell, the sacrifice of the young man, meshes with the figure of the Corn King or Year King made familiar by Sir James Frazer's *The Golden Bough*: the vigorous young man who marries the Earth Goddess and is sacrificed at the end of his short term, in imitation of the corn which springs up and is cut down. Modern scholars doubt if kings were sacrificed in fact rather than symbolically or ceremonially;[2] but it's a good story, and it's there in the back of a lot of fantasy writers' minds, I'm sure. Moreover, there's something sexy about a handsome young man in bondage to a cruel queen, and sexy goes down well in young adult fiction. We've got used to the idea; we take it for granted: Faeryland is ruled by a capricious, dangerous queen.

But once upon a time, Faeryland was ruled by kings, or else (since kings need wives) by kings and queens together, in which case, in a reflection of what people saw about them and regarded as the natural order, it was the king who was more important. Even in *A Midsummer Night's Dream*, where Titania and Oberon are equal enough in status that a quarrel between them spills over into the mortal world as dreadful weather, the balance nevertheless finally tips on Oberon's side: while the frame of the play is the marriage of Theseus to the Amazon queen Hippolyta, whom he has conquered in war.

Most people, however, would be hard put to name a fairy

Wynne Jones' *Fire and Hemlock*, Pamela Dean's *Tam Lin*, and Patricia McKillip's *Winter Rose*.

2 Dowden, Ken, *European Paganism*, Routledge 2000, 285.

king other than Oberon. Who were they, and why have they disappeared from popular culture and consciousness? How and why have the fairy queens taken over?

In the complicated Irish tale *The Wooing of Étain*,[3] Midir 'king of the elf mounds of Ireland', obtains the beautiful Étain for his partner and brings her home, where she incurs the enmity of his original wife 'the cunning woman' Fuamnach. Fuamnach transforms Étain into a puddle of water, from which she regenerates as a miraculous purple fly: 'Sweeter than pipes and harps and horns . . . was the sound of her voice and the hum of her wings.' But Fuamnach conjures a wind to blow the fly away. Étain is whirled on the wind for a thousand years, till at last she falls into the drinking cup of the wife of Etar, an Ulster hero, who swallows her and becomes pregnant. Étain is reborn and marries Eochaid, king of Ireland.

Midir is still searching for Étain, but now she is another man's wife. He sets out to win her from Eochaid by a series of wagers, in course of which he performs a number of mighty magical tasks. Finally he wins the right to put his arms around Étain and kiss her. Eochaid surrounds the couple with an army of his men.

> 'Do not blush, O Étain,' said Midir, 'it is not unwomanly of thee. I have been a year,' said he, 'seeking thee with gifts and treasures, not did I

---

3 *Tochmarc Étaine* or *The Wooing of Étain* is preserved in two Irish manuscripts of the early twelfth and fifteenth centuries, but on the evidence of the language the tale is thought to date from the eighth or ninth centuries.

> take thee until I had Eochaid's leave.' . . . 'I have told thee,' said she, 'that I will not go to thee unless Eochaid sell me. As for thou, thou mayst take me if Eochaid sell me.'
>
> 'I will not sell thee indeed,' said Eochaid, 'but let him put his arms around thee in the middle of the house as thou art.' 'It shall be done,' said Midir. He takes his weapons in his left hand, and the woman he took under his right arm, and he bore her away through the skylight of the house. The hosts rose up in shame around the king. They beheld two swans in flight round Tara.[4]

The lovers escape, and the shamed and angry Eochaid sets about digging up all the elf mounds of Ireland: fruitlessly, for 'what they would dig up one day would be restored on the morrow'. Nevertheless, the digging annoys Midir, who offers Eochaid a final chance to regain Étain, but only if he can pick her out from among fifty women all of her form and likeness.[5] Eochaid picks one whom he believes to be Étain, but he is mistaken: Étain was pregnant when Midir seized her, and the woman Eochaid has chosen is his own daughter. (Unluckily, he sleeps with her.) Étain herself will never come back.

What is this story all about? For the moment I will

---

4 *Tochmarc Étaine*, tr. and ed. Osborn Bergin and R.I. Best, *Eriu 12*, 185.

5 The motif in which a hero must identify a wife or princess from among a number of identical women, appears also in fairy tales such as *The Queen Bee*, KHM 62, and possibly in *Sir Orfeo*, as discussed below.

simply note that it includes themes of love, death, rebirth and substitution. Midir is a king of the elf mounds, a lord of the brugh: he comes from the underworld. He is immortal, but replaces his immortal fairy wife with the mortal Étain. Fuamnach attempts to kill Étain, who is reborn once as a fly and then after the passage of a thousand years, once more as a woman. Is she now immortal? Or touched by death? Or is that the same thing? Somehow Midir still has a claim to her even though she is married to Eochaid and doesn't remember her past life. 'Who art thou who has come to meet me?' she asks. 'What is thy name?' When Midir explains and asks, 'Wilt thou go with me?' she replies, 'I will not barter the king of Ireland for a man whose kindred and race I know not.' Yet the inevitable happens: Midir seizes her in the midst of the king's hall and they fly away as swans. 'Water birds possessed powerful symbolism in Celtic myths because they are at home in all elements: water, air and land.'[6] Because they mate for life, swans also symbolise love faithful unto death. Though the swans take to the air, Eochaid must dig the earth, grub up the elf mounds (which are graves) in his attempt to recover his wife, and Midir's last offer is a trick, another substitution. Eochaid no longer truly knows Étain; his memory of her is now unreliable. 'My wife is the best at serving drink in Ireland,' he declares. 'I shall recognise her by her serving.' Yet even as he chooses, he is unsure. 'This is Étain, and it is not herself.'

It has been suggested that *The Wooing of Étain* is one source for the early Middle English metrical romance *Sir Orfeo* which

---

6 Aldhouse-Green, Miranda, *The Celtic Myths*, 72.

includes some similar motifs, such as the disappearance of the queen from among ranks of armed men: but personally I doubt it. Such motifs are frequently to be found in Celtic tales and in any case the underlying point is not so much that Midir uses magic to escape with Étain, as that physical force is useless against the power of death. The kingdoms of death and faery are closely identified.

In *Sir Orfeo*, which blends Celtic and English fairy lore with the Greek myth of Orpheus, the fairy king must be Pluto, lord of the dead, though he is never named. One hot morning, Orfeo's queen, Dame Heurodis, falls asleep under 'a fair ympe-tre' (a grafted apple tree). She wakes in distress, having dreamed of a king accompanied by knights and ladies on white steeds, who has told her that on the morrow, she must come to live with him forever. Orfeo encircles her with his warriors, but to no avail: she is spirited away the very next day, as foretold, and 'Men wist neuer where she was bicome'.[7]

Desperate with grief, Orfeo lives like a wild man for some years, his harp his only consolation. Sometimes he sees the fairy hunt go by 'with dim cri & bloweing', or fairy knights and ladies dancing or riding. One day he recognises among them his own lost wife, but although the tears fall from her eyes on beholding him, she cannot utter a word. Orfeo follows as the procession passes through a rock into the underworld. Three miles underground he comes upon a crystal castle of a hundred towers. Enclosed within its walls is a gruesome collection of 'folk who were thought dead, but were not': some without heads,

7 *Sir Orfeo*, Auchinleck ms, line 194.

others maimed or wounded, some strangled, drowned, burned. (Middle English characters look strange if you're not used to them, but they're not that difficult to read. All you need is strong nerves and the information that þ = th as in 'thorn'; ȝ = gh as in 'sleigh' – a sort of 'yuh' sound; and v = u. But because many of the words are archaic, there's a prose translation below.)

> Wives þere lay on childe-bedde
> Sum dedde and sum awedde,
> & wonder fele þere lay besides;
> Riȝt as þai slepe her vndertides,
> Eche was þus in þis warld y-nome,
> Wiþ fairi thither y-come.
> Þer he seiȝe his owhen wiif
> Dame Heurodis, his lef liif,
> Slepe vnder an ympe-tre:
> Bi her cloþes he knewe þat it was he.[8]

('Wives lay there in child-bed, some dead and some mad: and wondrous many others lay there too: as they had fallen asleep at noon each was taken from this world and carried there by fairy magic. There he saw his own wife Dame Herodis, as dear to him as life, sleeping under a grafted tree: he knew her by her clothes.')

Disguised as a poor minstrel, Orfeo plays so well that the underworld king tells him to name his fee. Of course Orfeo

---

8 Op. cit., lines 399–408.

asks for his own wife: 'þat ich leuedi, briȝt on ble/þat slepeth vnder þe ympe-tre'[9]: 'that same lady, bright of face, who sleeps under the grafted tree'. Reluctantly the king consents and Orfeo succeeds in bringing Herodys out of the power of death and back to the world of the living.

The unknown medieval author of *Sir Orfeo* offers us, in presumably deliberate contrast to the canonical Greek tale of Orpheus and Eurydice, a happy ending. Yet it is still a dark story, full of suffering. What does it mean that this underground fairyland is full of people who 'were thought dead, but were not'? How can you not be dead if you are headless, drowned, strangled? When Orfeo sees his wife riding past with the fairy troop in our world, she appears as in life, though silent. He knows her at once, but the vision is like a memory. In the underworld, she is 'asleep' – as if preserved at the moment of death – and he can recognise her only by her clothes.[10] Like Eochaid, has Orfeo forgotten his wife's face?

The grafted apple tree under which Herodys dreams of the fairy king is itself a signifier of the Otherworld and so not the safest place to fall asleep. But which Otherworld? To the medieval mind there was a choice: even the Christian church offered at least three. In *Le Morte D'Arthur* Lancelot also falls asleep under an apple tree and is carried off by Morgan le Fay and three other queens to the Castle Chariot,[11] where they

---

9 Op. cit., lines 405–8.

10 *Sir Orfeo*, Auchinleck ms, line 408. Or is this a test, as in *The Wooing of Étain*? If you can recognise the dead, perhaps you can bring them back?

11 Malory, Thomas, *Le Morte D'Arthur*, Book VI Chapter 3: the other three queens are the Queen of Northgales, the Queen of Eastland

lay him 'in a chamber cold' and demand his love. The Isle of Avalon, to which Morgan and some of the same queens later convey the wounded Arthur,[12] is 'the island of apple trees', and Malory tells us that he does not know if Arthur is dead or alive.

> Yet some men say in many parts that King Arthur is not dead, but had by the will of our Lord Jesu into another place; and men say that he shall come again, and he shall win the holy cross. I will not say that it shall be so, but rather I will say, here in this world he changed his life. But many men say that there is written upon his tomb this verse: HIC IACET ARTHURUS, REX QUONDAM REXQUE FUTURUS.[13]

Where is this 'other place'? It is a space defined by what it is not: not heaven, not hell, not purgatory, not earth. Fairyland lies down the alternative road, the green and ferny road the Queen of Elphame indicates to Thomas Rhymer in the ballad. Thus, Arthur too may claim to be a fairy king. He is not exactly dead, but sleeping in the island valley of the apple trees, or in a deep cave surrounded by his knights. One day he will wake: but it won't be in our time, and we mustn't expect to see it.

The Welsh underworld of Annwfn[14] was ruled by King

---

and the Queen of the Out Isles – non-existent fairy places, all.

12 Op. cit., Book XXI Chapter 6: this time the queens include the Queen of Northgales, the Queen of the Waste Land, and Nimue, 'the chief lady of the lake'.

13 Op. cit., Book XXI, Chapter 7.

14 'Derived from *an* (in, inside) + *dwfn* ("world")': *The Mabinogion*, tr.

Arawn, whom Pwyll Prince of Dyfed meets in the *Mabinogion*. After an incident out stag-hunting, the mortal Pwyll offers recompense to Arawn for having driven his white-coated, red-eared fairy hounds away from the quarry in favour of his own pack. In a bargain similar to that of *Gawain and the Green Knight*,[15] King Arawn suggests an identity swap: Pwyll is to take Arawn's place in his kingdom, and at the end of the year must face and fight Arawn's enemy King Hafgan.

> 'I will set thee in Annwn in my stead, and the fairest lady thou didst ever see I will set to sleep with thee each night, and my form and semblance upon thee, so that [no man] shall know that thou art not I. And that,' said he, 'till the end of a year from tomorrow, and our tryst then in this very place.'[16]

Like Gawain, Pwyll is courteous and canny enough to refrain from sexual intercourse with the beautiful lady, who is of course Arawn's wife: 'the moment they got into bed, he turned his face to the bedside and his back towards her . . . not a single night to the year's end was different from what that first night was.' At the end of the year he rides to the ford, meets King Hafgan and strikes the single blow that fells him 'with a mortal

---

Sioned Davies, 228.

15 Though the Green Knight is never actually identified as a fairy king, he is arguably an example of one, and the Green Chapel certainly resembles a hollow hill, barrow or *brugh* – see lines 2178–2184.

16 *The Mabinogion*, tr. and ed. Gwyn Jones and Thomas Jones, 4.

wound'. These proofs of faith impress Arawn, and thenceforth he and Pwyll are friends.

Fairy kings seem to have a predilection for threesomes. The theme of a woman shared with or disputed between rivals – Arawn, his lady and Pwyll: Midir, Étain and Eochaid: Pluto, Herodys and Orfeo – appears again in the tale *Culhwch and Olwen* from the *Mabinogion*. The hero Gwyn ap Nudd, later known as king of the Welsh fairies, abducts the maiden Creiddylad from her lover Gwythyr. A vicious war breaks out between the two heroes, and hearing of it:

> Arthur . . . came into the North, and summoned to him Gwyn son of Nudd . . . and peace was made between Gwyn son of Nudd and Gwythyr son of Greidawl. This is the peace that was made: the maiden should remain in her father's house, unmolested by either side, and there should be battle between Gwyn and Gwythyr every May-calends for ever and ever, from that day till Doomsday, and the one of them that should be victor on Doomsday, let him have the maiden.[17]

Caught in this unresolved and never-ending conflict, it's no wonder Gwyn ap Nudd is also named as a lord of the Wild Hunt, leading 'the *Cwn Annwn*, the Hounds of the Other

---

17 'Culhwch and Olwen', *The Mabinogion*, ed. Gwyn Jones, Thomas Jones, 128/9.

World, over Cader Idris"[18] every Halloween, and announcing in a dialogue poem from the *Black Book of Carmarthen*, 'I am the escort of the grave'.[19] As for Pwyll, probably it's wise for a mortal to avoid sleeping with the wife of the king of the underworld: as queen of the dead, she may herself be dead. What would have been the penalty if Pwyll had been less wise? We're not told, but the stakes could be high. If Sir Gawain had given in to temptation and slept with Bertilak's wife, would the Green Knight have slain him?

In a legend related by the twelfth-century courtier Walter Map, a British king called Herla meets an unnamed, goat-footed pygmy king who rules underground halls of unutterable splendour and – perhaps ominously – announces himself to be 'King over many kings and princes, an unnumbered and innumerable people'. (The dead are innumerable . . .) The pygmy foretells Herla's marriage and suggests 'that I shall first attend your wedding and you mine on the same day a year hence'. Like Pwyll, like Gawain, Herla is bound by the bargain. He follows the pygmy into fairyland:

> The party entered a cave in a high cliff, and after an interval of darkness, passed, in a light which seemed to proceed not from sun or moon, but from a multitude of lamps, to the mansion of the pigmy. Here the wedding was celebrated . . . and when leave was granted, Herla departed laden

---

18 Rhys, John, *Celtic Folklore*, 203.
19 Squire, Charles, *Celtic Myth and Legend*, 258.

with gifts and presents of horses, dogs [and] hawks . . . The pigmy then escorted them as far as the place where darkness began, and then presented the king with a small blood-hound to carry, strictly enjoining him that on no account must any of his train dismount until that dog leapt from the arms of his bearer . . . Within a short space Herla arrived once more at the light of the sun and at his kingdom, where he accosted an old shepherd and asked for news of his Queen, naming her. The shepherd gazed at him in astonishment and said: 'Sir, I can hardly understand your speech, for you are a Briton and I a Saxon, but they say . . . that long ago, there was a Queen of that name over the very ancient Britons, who was the wife of King Herla; and he, the story says, disappeared in company with a pigmy at this very cliff, and was never seen on earth again . . .

The king, who thought he had made a stay of but three days, could scarce sit his horse for amazement. Some of his company, forgetting the pigmy's orders, dismounted before the dog had alighted, and in a moment fell into dust. Whereupon the king . . . warned the rest under pain of a like fate not to touch the earth before the alighting of the dog. The dog has not yet alighted. And the story says that this King Herla

> still holds on his mad course with his band in eternal wanderings, without stop or stay.[20]

Having once disappeared into the pygmy king's underground kingdom, Herla is to all intents and purposes dead himself, lost to his people and displaced in time. There is no real way back from fairyland.

Also pygmy-sized is the fairy king Auberon in the French romance *Huon de Bordeaux*. He is a dwarf with the face of a beautiful child – whose name resurfaces in *A Midsummer Night's Dream*. Here he is, in the sixteenth-century translation by Lord Berners who was Governor of Calais for Henry VIII and whiled away his spare time translating French histories and romances. The hero of the tale, Sir Huon, is journeying to Babylon (itself an almost magical city), when he is warned of the dangers of a magical wood:

> I counsell you to take the long way, for yf ye take the shorter way ye must passe throwout a wood a xvi leges of length; but the way is so full of the fayrey & of straunge thynges, that such as passe that way are lost, for in that wood abideth a kynge of the fayrey namyd Oberon / he is of height but of iii fote, and crokyd shulderyd, but yet he hath an aungelkyke visage, so that there is no mortall man that seethe him but that taketh grete pleasure to beholde his fase / and ye shall

20 Map, Walter, *De Nugis Curialium*, tr. M.R. James, 13–16.

> no soner be enteryd into that wood, yf ye go that way / he wyll fynde the maner to speke with you / and yf ye speke to hym ye are lost for euer . . .[21]

'And if you speak to him you are lost forever . . .' Oberon haunts a fairy wood, and so sometimes does Gwyn ap Nudd,[22] but most of these fairy kings rule underground lands, and there is a pervading sense of loss that hangs about them. Their glittering palaces are illusions, their lands are lands of shadow. Moreover, there's an interesting hint in all of these stories of *substitution*, of succession. Pwyll *becomes* Arawn for a whole year, and is afterwards so closely identified with him in friendship that his name is changed to Pwyll Pen Annwfn, 'Pwyll Chief of Annwfn'. After visiting the pygmy king's halls, Herla finds himself hundreds of years in the future. He cannot dismount from his horse without crumbling to dust, and therefore still rides the Welsh border hills at the head of his troop of knights. The pygmy king vanishes from the tale forever: in some sense, Herla has replaced him.

Except for Oberon (who claims to be the son of the Lady of the Secret Isle and Julius Caesar, and who has a place reserved for him in Paradise), these fairy kings are mostly pagan, or at least outside the Christian order: there is no sense that they will ever attain heaven. At Oberon's death, in another substitution, Duke Huon and his wife Esclaramond become

---

21 *Huon of Burdeux, done into English by Sir John Bourchier, Lord Berners*, ed. S.L. Lee, 63.

22 *Medieval Folklore: An Encyclopaedia*, ed. Lindahl, McNamara, Lindow, 190.

King and Queen of Faeryland – much to the wrath of King Arthur, who hoped to succeed. What then becomes of Huon's immortal soul? Rudyard Kipling offers an answer: Huon's story is behind this fabulous piece of writing in his story 'Weland's Sword':

> 'Butterfly wings, indeed! I've seen Sir Huon and a troop of his people setting out from Tintagel Castle for Hy-Brasil in the teeth of a sou-westerly gale, with the spray flying all over the Castle, and Horses of the Hills wild with fright. Out they'd go in a lull, screaming like gulls, and back they'd be driven five good miles inland before they could come head to wind again. Butterfly wings! It was Magic – Magic as black as Merlin could make it, and the whole sea was green fire and white foam with singing mermaids in it. And the Horses of the Hills picked their way from one wave to another by the lightning flashes. *That* was how it was in the old days!'[23]

In a companion story, *Cold Iron*, Puck tells the children about 'Sir Huon of Bordeaux – he succeeded King Oberon. He had been a bold knight once, but he was lost on the road to Babylon, a long while back . . .'[24] I believe Kipling is suggesting the loss both of Huon's identity and of his Christian soul.

---

23 Kipling, Rudyard, 'Weland's Sword', *Puck of Pook's Hill*, 14.
24 Kipling, Rudyard, 'Cold Iron', *Rewards and Fairies*, 9.

In a tale known as *The Sons of the Dead Wife*, Walter Map tells of a Breton knight who buried his wife and 'long after her death went on mourning for her'. Then:

> He found her at night in a great company of women in a valley in a wide tract of desert. He marvelled and was afraid, and when he saw her whom he had buried, alive again, he could not trust his eyes, and doubted what the fairies (fates) could be doing. He resolved to capture her . . . [and] accordingly seized her, and enjoyed a union with her for many years . . . and had children by her, whose descendants are numerous at this day, and are called the sons of the dead mother. This would be an incredible and portentous breach of nature's laws, did not some evidence of its truth exist.[25]

Unlike Eochaid, this unnamed knight manages to recognise his wife among the 'great company of women' and like Sir Orfeo, succeeds in bringing her out of the gloomy land of death. He is fortunate. Fairyland is a place so close to hell that the inhabitants have to pay tithes to the Devil every seven years. The mortal inhabitants are lost to us, yet may be glimpsed any time on twilight lanes or wandering on grassy mounds. You cannot rescue someone from heaven or hell, but tantalisingly, the dead in fairyland may not be quite gone, only stolen away

---

25 Map, Walter, *De Nugis Curialium*, tr. M.R. James, 189.

into some other dimension, some fairy realm of suspended half-existence, and perhaps they can be brought back. This is the fantasy of grief. And of course time runs differently there: if you visit, you risk losing yourself forever. Perhaps this tells us something about the danger of being trapped in grief, unable to move on.

I wrote on this theme, and the mysterious underground kingdom of the dead or half-dead, in my children's fantasy *Dark Angels*. One of the characters, the troubadour knight Lord Hugo, lost his wife seven years before the book opens.

> 'The night she died – it was New Year's Eve, and the candles burned so low and blue, and we heard over and over again the sound of thunder. That was the *Mesnie Furieuse* – the Wild Host – riding over the valleys. Between the old year and the new, between life and death – don't you think, when the soul is loosening from the body, the elves can steal it?'[26]

So I sent my young hero Wolf searching for Hugo's lost wife through the cramped tunnels of the old lead mines under the local mountain, Devil's Edge, to confront the lord of the underworld himself, who tells him:

> 'The old mad beggars on the roads, they're my people. The cast-off children nobody wants. The

26 Langrish, Katherine, *Dark Angels*, 102.

> babies abandoned in ditches. The guilty, the lost, the wanderers, the refuse of Heaven – they all come down to me, to crawl into this crack in God's creation where they can wrap a few rags of make-believe around them to keep warm.' His voice sank to a whisper. 'Heaven has forgotten us, and for one little payment every seven years, Hell turns a blind eye.'[27]

If kings of fairyland are lords of the dead, so too are its queens. Sir Walter Scott summarises what happens in the medieval metrical romance of *Thomas of Erceldoune* when Thomas kisses the fairy queen:

> The change which ensues in her person is strikingly painted. Her bright eyes become dead; her fair locks drop from the naked scalp; her rich raiment is changed into rags, repentance and terror were like unavailing: he was compelled to bid adieu 'to sun and moon, to grass and every green tree,' and to leave the earth with his supernatural conductor. He mounts behind her on her palfrey and they journey . . . through the realms of utter darkness, hearing only the roaring of waters, through which they sometimes seem to cross.[28]

27 Op. cit., 326.
28 *Sir Tristem, A Metrical Romance of the Thirteenth Century by Thomas of Erceldoune, called The Rhymer*, ed. Sir Walter Scott, 18.

The better-known ballad of Thomas the Rhymer, which Scott considered a copy of this poem, modernised by an English hand and dating from around 1700, leaves out this transformation of the queen into what seems as much corpse as hag – but leaves no doubt at all of the Otherworld nature of the journey:

> O they rade on, and further on
> And they waded through rivers aboon the knee,
> And they saw neither sun nor moon,
> But they heard the roaring of the sea.
>
> It was mirk, mirk night and there was nae stern
> light
> And they waded through red blude to the knee;
> For a' the blude that's shed on earth
> Rins through the springs o' that countrie.[29]

In the romance, Thomas and the Queen pass by the gates of Paradise and the Queen warns Thomas not to touch the fruit of the Tree of Knowledge. In the ballad, she offers him an apple from 'a garden green' which gives him the undesirable gift of a tongue that cannot lie. In either case, here again are apples of the Otherworld. Yet the theme of loss, of desperate, unassuaged grief that runs through so many of the narratives I've been looking at – that seems missing.

So where have all the fairy kings gone?

---

29 'Thomas the Rhymer', *The Oxford Book of Ballads*, ed. James Kinsley, 8.

To the medieval mind, fairyland was useful. It provided breathing space, wriggle-room in a universe otherwise too well planned, for men and women who perhaps felt uncomfortably visible under the eye of all-seeing God. Fairies, as C.S. Lewis remarks, 'soften the classic severity of the huge design. They intrude a welcome hint of wildness and uncertainly into a universe that is in danger of becoming a little too self-explanatory'.[30] Worse than heaven but a great deal better than hell, fairyland was a place where you could imagine your not-very-worthy dead neighbour ending up, or the wife who died in childbed unshriven, or your unbaptised baby, to whom even Purgatory was officially closed. It offered a little desperate hope, too. You couldn't bring anyone back from heaven or hell, but from fairyland? There were enough stories to suggest that there might be just a chance.

The Reformation officially did away with at least one Otherworld – Purgatory – but fairyland was unaddressed by dogma, and so it lingered on. By the late sixteenth century however, the fairies were becoming more and more associated with witchcraft. When Thomas the Rhymer mistakes the beautiful fairy queen for the Queen of Heaven, she disabuses him: 'That name does not belong to me.' But a fairy king – who might a fairy king resemble?

Andro Man, tried at Aberdeen in 1597, claimed to have been visited as a child by not only the fairy queen, but Satan in the guise of an angel calling himself Christsonday. 'The queen has a grip of all the craft, but Christsonday is the gudeman and

---

30 Lewis, C.S., *The Discarded Image*, 122.

has all power under God.'[31] Christsonday would run with the fairy queen in the guise of a stag, and Andro believed himself to have seen 'the king who died at Flodden' and Thomas the Rhymer in their company. 'We are in elfland, but the cloven hoof is showing itself.'[32] In late twelfth-century Britain, Walter Map could write, without any apparent concern over possible diabolic origins, of a goat-footed pygmy king. Four hundred years later, Otherworld males were no longer likely to be identified as kings. Their place had been usurped by the Devil.

There is one last place where fairy kings may be found. They still appear in folklore and in fiction as leaders of the Wild Hunt: to the best of my knowledge all the British Wild Hunts are led by men. There's King Herla and Wild Edric in Shropshire, Sir Francis Drake in Devon, and King Arthur himself gallops past in a flashing snatch of sixteenth-century Scots verse: 'Arthour knycht he raid on nycht viтht giltin spur and candil lycht'[33] ('Arthur knight, he rode at night with gilten spur and candle light'). To see the Wild Huntsman is an omen of death or calamity, but the Hunt is by definition itinerant, its deathly participants 'imprisoned in the viewless winds/And blown with restless violence round about the pendant world'.[34] Leaders of the Wild Hunt do not sit enthroned; they are outcasts, exiles. There are no more Kings of Fairyland.

---

31 Macculloch, Canon J.A., 'The Mingling of Witch and Fairy Beliefs in Sixteenth and Seventeenth Century Scotland', *Folk-Lore, Vol 32*, December 1921, 227–244.

32 Ibid.

33 *The Complaynt of Scotland*, ed. John Leyden, 98.

34 Shakespeare, William, *Measure for Measure*, Act 3, Scene 1.

Naming the King of the Fairies, or How to Get Out of the Hill

His fair face is so still and calm
You never would think he means you harm.
If he sets his hand on the bridle-rein
Your horse will start away, away –
See! Full of crows the turning sky
As on the straight ley road you lie.
Under the hill the air is dark,
The smells are all of mould and clay,
He'll show you where the dead men are,
And like a child, lead you away.
Young Roland blew his ox's horn
To make the Dark Tower tumble down –
But here he stays with Helen and John:
They toss a gilded ball and play.
You and the dark young man look on,
But never a word they say.

He leads you on, he leads you down
Until you come to great Troy Town.
The walls are low, not three feet high –
Along you dance, for you must try
To find the fountain in the dark
That wells up from the centre mark.
The mazing streets are not too wide
(Sing sweetly in the dry, black air)
They press you in on either side –
You're at the fountain, in the square.
The darkness snuffles like a mole.
You'll never leave or find your home
If once you drink from that stone bowl,
But leaning on the fountain there
The dark young man will have you whole –
You'll stay until your bones are bare.

He takes your wrist, and on you go
To earthworm tunnels far below,
You taste the clay, you taste the marl,
Those fairy ferns are stamped in coal.
Now you're in trouble, sure as fate,
Shouldering the hill's demanding weight.
Don't lose your nerve or feel despair
If you want to be free in the windy air.
He'll loose your hand and go away,
He'll leave you cramped and buried here:
You'll choke your life out far from day
If once you falter, faint with fear.

It's breathless-black, you're wrapped in earth,
Your mouth is clogged, you dream of death –
Pull from his grip and think of birth!
Say, 'King Arawn, I will not stay!'
He'll lift you to his roof of turf
And out you'll stand on the ley

Colour in fairy tales

It's usual for collections of fairy tales to include pictures. When I was small, the simple retellings I was able to read had sumptuous full-page illustrations by Rene Cloke in naïve primary-school colours – bright scarlets, sky blues, pastel pinks, egg-yolk yellows and grass greens. As I grew older I read Andrew Lang's Colour Fairy Books, interspersed with plates by H. J. Ford in hot reds and strong violets, midnight blues and burnt-toffee umbers. Hans Christian Andersen's tales came arrayed with Edmund Dulac's graceful watercolours in twilight blues, underwater greens, pale ochres, shadowy purples. And Grimms' fairy tales seemed perfectly represented by Arthur Rackham's strong inky woods and midnight skies: all rusty browns, glimmering blues, and greens so deep they are almost black.

But fairy stories don't *need* illustrations. Intended originally to be listened to rather than read, they contain their own colours, brilliant as any illuminated manuscript. As red as blood, as black as ebony, as white as snow.

In his book *An Experiment in Criticism*, C.S. Lewis talks

about good and bad writing and the possible differences between them. He suggests that some readers prefer bad writing because they do not want or are not interested in the things which good writing can provide: richness of experience, for example, or depth of thought. Some readers simply want the action, the page-turning, the next thing. And this explains the popularity of the airport thriller, and of Dan Brown.

For such a reader, Lewis says, good writing will be either too rich or too bare for his purposes.

> A woodland scene by DH Lawrence or a mountain valley by Ruskin gives him far more than he knows what to do with; on the other hand, he would be disappointed with Malory's 'he arrived afore a postern opened towards the sea, and was open without any keeping, save two lions kept the entry, and the moon shone clear.' Nor would he be content with 'I was terribly afraid' instead of 'my blood ran cold'. To the good reader's imagination such statements of the bare facts are often the most evocative of all. But the moon shining clear is not enough for the unliterary. They would rather be told that the castle was 'bathed in a flood of silver moonlight'.[1]

I'm not concerned here with Lewis's thesis about different types of reading – I think he's right, but I also think all of us

---

1 Lewis, C.S., *An Experiment in Criticism*, 33.

can be 'good' and 'bad' readers: I have days when I can be that attentive, sensitive reader Lewis applauds and other days when I am simply too lazy. But I do want to point out that fairy tales – traditional fairy tales – tend to be sparse on description.

> Once upon a time there was a princess who went out into the forest and sat down at the edge of a cool well. She had a golden ball that was her favorite plaything. She threw it up high and caught it in the air and was delighted by all this.[2]

This is the beginning of *The Frog King* in the 1812 version of Grimms' *Children's and Household Tales*. It is certainly not overwritten. There are just two adjectives. The well is cool, the ball is golden; Lewis's careful reader will infer that (since the princess seeks out a cool well in a forest) the day must be hot and the ball is precious. It's really all we need to know, but Wilhelm Grimm couldn't leave it at that, so by 1857 the revised story opens more descriptively:

> In olden times, when wishing still helped one, there lived a king whose daughters were all beautiful, but the youngest was so beautiful that the sun itself, which has seen so much, was astonished whenever it shone on her face. Close by the King's castle lay a great dark forest, and

---

2 'The Frog King, or Iron Henry', *The Original Folk and Fairy Tales of the Brothers Grimm*, ed. Jack Zipes, 13.

> under an old lime-tree in the forest was a well, and when the day was very warm, the King's child went out into the forest and sat down by the side of the cool fountain; and when she was bored she took a golden ball, and threw it up on high and caught it.[3]

I sympathise with Wilhelm's impulse to improve upon his source. 'Earlier' doesn't necessarily mean 'more authentic', and it certainly doesn't have to mean 'better'. I rather like this leisurely, more literary opening. The passage has accumulated several more adjectives, but they are in keeping with traditional style. Lovely as it is, the phrase 'so beautiful that the sun was astonished' tells us nothing about what the king's daughter actually looks like. No modern writer who might wish to turn *The Frog King* into a novel would be able to resist the temptation to give us much, much more. The princess would acquire a name and a personal history. We would learn what colour her hair and eyes are, whether her nose turns up at the end, what clothes she wears. My imaginary author would feel compelled to visualise the well and describe to the reader – 'Show, don't tell!' – its carved marble parapet or rustic stone wall. Such details soon begin to clutter up the narrative. As the story turns into an extended, elaborate fantasy (however good of its kind) it ceases to be a fairy tale.

A fairy tale doesn't try too hard. In keeping everything simple, it also keeps everything fresh. 'Close by the King's

---

3 'The Frog-King, or Iron Henry', KHM 1, *Grimm's Fairy Tales*, 17.

castle lay a great, dark forest' leaves almost everything to your imagination, and then comes the 'old lime tree' and the cool well, and that's as much as anyone needs to know.

Yet in what way is a phrase like 'green as grass' or 'black as coal' less of a cliché than 'bathed in a flood of silver moonlight'? Used sparingly, such similes are not clichés because they are so simple. They leave the imagination free. 'Red as blood'. The colour flashes on the inward eye in all its familiar, potent brilliance – and is gone. What else can 'red' be as red as? Strain after a comparison as much as you like, you'll do no better.

Colours in fairy tales are strong, simple, basic, and meaningful:

> Once upon a time in the middle of winter, when the flakes of snow were falling like feathers from the sky, a Queen sat at a window sewing, and the frame of the window was made of black ebony. And whilst she was sewing and looking out of the window at the snow, she pricked her finger with the needle, and three drops of blood fell upon the snow. And the red looked pretty on the white snow, and she thought to herself, 'Would that I had a child as white as snow, as red as blood, and as black as the wood of the window-frame.'[4]

You don't get pink in fairy tales, you don't get purple. Yellow is rare. But there is white snow, white linen, white snakes, white

4 'Little Snow-White', KHM 53, *Grimm's Fairy Tales*, 249.

doves, white swans, white feathers. There is red blood, and roses as red as blood. Green is not often named, but is to be found in grass, rushes, hazel branches, nettles, and is implicit in the background of dark forests. There are black bulls, black ravens – black ebony, coal, pitch. Golden hair, golden straw, golden crowns, golden spinning wheels.

> The dove said to her, 'For seven years must I fly about the world, but at every seventh step that you take I will let fall a drop of red blood and a white feather, and these will show you the way.'[5]

White, black and red are meaningful colours because they are rare in nature and therefore noticeable. White is the colour of innocence, the colour of an untrodden fall of snow under which a whole landscape is transformed. A white dove is an emblem of peace, a black raven a signifier of wisdom – or death. In some variants of *Snow-White*, it is a raven which the queen sees against the snow, more likely and a sharper contrast than an ebony window-frame. Black is unusual. Most birds are brownish: even today with our dulled attention to nature, we notice black crows and white swans. Before the invention of chemical dyes, black was a very expensive colour for clothes. It stood out: most people could not afford to wear it. And red of course is the most meaningful of all colours, the most emotionally charged. Red is the colour that accompanies childbirth, wounds, war, accidents. Red is the stuff of life and death.

---

5 'The Singing, Soaring Lark', KHM 88, *Grimm's Fairy Tales*, 399.

Silver is the colour of the unattainable moon and stars. Gold is the colour of the sun; or perhaps it should be the other way around: the sun is more glorious than gold. Both silver and gold are precious and desirable. The princess in *The Singing, Soaring Lark* wears a dress 'as brilliant as the sun itself', while the heroine of *The Black Bull of Norroway* cracks open nuts to reveal dresses the colour of the sun, moon and stars. Yellow, the colour of so many common flowers, is nevertheless rare in fairy tales and when it does appear, it is ominous. In Madame d'Aulnoy's *The Yellow Dwarf*, the yellow-faced, yellow-clad 'little monster' brings disaster and death upon two unhappy lovers. Blue, the colour of the sky, is also strangely rare. Apart from the eerie, supernatural *blue light* – the witch-light – in the story of that name, the only instance I can find is in a sad little tale about a toad, and refers to an artificial object, a handkerchief:

> An orphan child was sitting by the town wall spinning, when she saw a paddock [toad] coming out of a hole low down in the wall. Swiftly she spread out beside it one of the blue silk handkerchiefs for which paddocks have such a liking, and which are the only things on which they will creep. As soon as the paddock saw it, it went back, then returned, bringing with it a small golden crown . . .[6]

---

6 'Tales of the Paddock', KHM 105, *Grimm's Fairy Tales*, 480.

Colours in fairy tales aren't decoration; they aren't even 'just' descriptive. They carry information, they are a form of emphasis, and they can be relied upon. A golden head which rises to the surface of a well *will* be magical, *will* aid you, if you know how to behave towards it. A girl who owns a dress as golden as the sun, or who can ask a hazel tree to shake gold and silver down upon her, will always prove fortunate. White doves aid the innocent and peck out the eyes of the guilty.

Here's a poem into which I tried to work the colours of fairy tales.

Consulting the Yellow Dwarf

Out from the pine forest stepped
the bowing yellow dwarf, and stopped the prince,
who – half despairing – told him everything.

If the bent woman, walking backwards, sets you
to sweep the green pins with an old owl's feather,
and call up storm clouds in the fine June weather,
and ride the yellow colt of your last nightmare –
what can you do but sigh and tell your story
to the first kindly stranger who has met you?

'Tell me,' the dwarf said, 'what of your princess?'
'Oh, turned into a brown thrush long ago
she sits and sings in a fine gilded cage,
and every spring she lays a pure blue egg,
which, hatched, displays a tiny golden crown.
That's why you see me wandering alone,
for hills of glass and plains of knives spring up
behind, and hinder me from turning back.'

'Where's your white horse? Your squire, young
Constant Jack?'

'Jack used to fret me – always making speed.
He rode my white horse red towards the wars
a long time back. Today, I have no doubt,
sheep graze the fine new grass between their
bones.'

'Ah,' said the dwarf. 'And so you're quite alone?'

'Alone. And burdened with confusing tasks.'

Then, pointing where the green ride ducked and
dipped
to twist behind the dense pine barrier:
'Now,' said the dwarf, smiling, 'keep on till
dark . . .'

Thou shalt not ride sunwise about Tara

'*Geasa*' – the magical prohibitions or tabus laid upon Irish heroes such as Cú Chulainn – must have been very difficult and frustrating to endure, especially since it seems to have been the fate of most heroes eventually to violate them.[1]

You remember how the young Setanta, son of Sualtim, gained the name Cú Chulainn ('Chulainn's Hound'), after killing the fierce guard-dog belonging to the smith Chulainn? When Chulainn complains of his hound's death, the boy offers to make it up to him:

> 'If there is a whelp of the same breed to be had in Ireland, I will rear him and train him until he is as good a hound as the one killed, and until that time, Chulainn,' he said, 'I myself will be your

1 Difficult to pronounce as well, for those of us who are not Irish, but I believe the approximate pronunciation for *geas* is 'geesh'.

> watch-dog, to guard your goods and your cattle and your house."[2]

After that, Cú Chulainn is laid under two *geasa*: never to eat the flesh of a dog, and never to refuse a meal offered to him by a woman. At the end of his life, when he is riding out to fight against Maeve's great army, these *geasa* are used against him by three witches as deadly as those in *Macbeth*:

> After a while he saw three hags, and they blind of the left eye, before him in the road, and they having a venomous hound they were cooking with charms on rods of the rowan tree. And he was going by them, for he knew it was not for his good they were there.
>
> But one of the hags called to him, 'Stop a while with us, Cuchulain.' 'I will not stop with you,' said Cuchulain. 'That is because we have nothing better than a dog to give you,' said the hag. 'If we had a grand, big cooking hearth, you would stop and visit us, but because it is only a little that we have, you will not stop.'
>
> [. . .] Then he went over to her, and she gave him the shoulder-blade of the hound out of her left hand, and he ate it out of his left hand. And he put it down on his left thigh, and the hand that took it was struck down, and the thigh he

---

2 *Cuchulain of Muirthemne*, tr. Lady Augusta Gregory, 11.

> put it on was struck through and through, so that the strength that was in them before left them.[3]

It couldn't be more ominous and presently, in forlorn battle against the odds, Cú Chulainn is mortally wounded and straps himself to a standing stone west of the lake of Muirthemne so that he will not meet his death lying down: and his horse, the Grey of Macha, defends him with its teeth and hooves until at last the hero dies and the crows descend upon him. Fans of *The Weirdstone of Brisingamen* will note that Alan Garner has used this scene for the death of the dwarf Durathror, who straps himself to the pillar of Clulow, defending Colin and Susan from the morthbrood.[4]

In another part of the Ulster cycle, *The Destruction of Dá Derga's Hostel*, King Conaire (Conaire Mór), whose father was a magical bird-man, is placed under a truly startling variety of *geasa*:

> 'Thou shalt not go righthandwise round Tara and lefthandwise around Bregia. The evil-beasts of Cerna must not be hunted by thee. And thou shalt not go out every ninth night beyond Tara. Thou shalt not sleep in a house from which firelight is manifest outside, after sunset, and in which (light) is manifest from without. And three Reds shall not go before thee to Red's house. And

---

3 *Cuchulain of Muirthemne*, tr. Lady Augusta Gregory, 335.
4 Garner, Alan, *The Weirdstone of Brisingamen*, 216.

> no rapine shall be wrought in thy reign. And after sunset a company of one woman or one man shall not enter the house in which thou art. And thou shalt not settle the quarrel of thy two thralls.'[5]

Of course, one by one Conaire breaks all the *geasa.* He goes out to make peace between two of his subject lords, he travels the wrong way around Tara and Bregia to avoid raiders; he hunts the beasts of Cerna without realising what they are. The country goes up in a cloud of smoke and fire, and:

> They that made of the world that smoky mist of magic were elves, and they did so because Conaire's tabus had been violated.[6]

At last, on his way to find shelter in the hostelry of his friend Dá Derga of Leinster, with its seven doors, Conaire sees three red horsemen riding ahead of him.

> Three red bucklers they bore, and three red spears were in their hands: three red steeds they bestrode, and three red heads of hair were on them. Red were they all, both body and hair and raiment, both steeds and men.[7]

Knowing another *geas* has been broken, Conaire sends his young

---

5 *The Destruction of Dá Derga's Hostel*, tr. Whitely Stokes, 27.
6 Op. cit., 33.
7 *The Destruction of Dá Derga's Hostel*, tr. Whitely Stokes, 36.

son Lefriflaith after the men to ask who they are. Lefriflaith calls out to them three times, and the third time one of them calls back that they are three of the Sidhe, banished from the elfmounds:

> 'Lo, my son, great the news. Weary are the steeds we ride. We ride the steeds of Donn Tetscorach from the elf-mounds. Though we are alive we are dead. Great are the signs: destruction of life: sating of ravens: feeding of crows, strife of slaughter: wetting of sword-edge, shields with broken bosses in hours after sundown. Lo, my son!'[8]

Conaire's last two *geasa* are broken when a sinister, lone woman comes to the door of Dá Derga's hostel (or inn):

> She came and leaned up against the doorpost, and she threw an evil eye upon the king and the young men about him. 'Well, woman,' said Conaire, 'if you have the Druid sight, what is it you see for us?' 'It is what I see for you,' she said, 'that nothing of your skin or of your flesh shall escape from the place you are in, except what the birds will bring away in their claws. And let me come into the house now.'[9]

---

8 Op. cit., 39.

9 *Cuchulain of Muirthemne*, tr. Lady Augusta Gregory, 93.

Greatly unwilling, the king allows the woman to enter, though not unnaturally, 'none of them felt easy in their minds after what she had said'. Finally, firelight from the hostel is spotted by Conaire's enemy, Ingcel the One-Eyed and his army of reivers. They attack, great destruction is wrought, and Conaire dies with his men.

A last example, just as ill-fated, is the *geasa* placed on Diarmuid by Gráinne, daughter of King Cormac and the promised bride of Finn MacCool. At the wedding feast Gráinne falls in love with one of his warriors, young Diarmuid. After sending Finn a cup that makes all who drink of it fall asleep, she asks Diarmuid to marry her, and when he refuses, she says,

> 'I place thee under geasa, and under the bonds of heavy druidical spells – bonds that true heroes never break through, that thou take me for thy wife before Finn and the others awaken from their sleep; and save me from this hateful marriage.'
>
> And Dermat, still unyielding, replied, 'Evil are those geasa thou hast put on me; and evil, I fear, will come of them.'[10]

He asks those of his friends whom Gráinne has not put to sleep what he should do. All agree he must comply with the *geas* even if it results in his death – which of course it eventually

10 Joyce, P.W., *Old Celtic Romances*, 191.

does, though not before many others have died first. Wounded by a boar at the end of the tale, Diarmuid explains to Finn that Gráinne 'put me under heavy geasa, which for all the wealth of the world I would not break', and begs Finn to save his life with a drink of water cupped in his healing hands. Thinking of Gráinne, Finn spills the water three times and Diarmuid dies.

So what were *geasa* all about? Were they ever a part of real life? Or were they simply a poetical, literary device? If they ever had any real currency, could anyone use them? If so, how often? How carelessly? Could you do the equivalent of putting your children under *geasa* to pick up their socks and tidy their rooms? Or would that kind of thing backfire just as badly as most of them seem to have done in the tales? *Geasa* seem to have been impossible to refuse, however arbitrary or awkward they might be.

In a note at the back of his translation of *Old Celtic Romances*, P.W. Joyce comments:

> Geasa means solemn vows, conjurations, injunctions, prohibitions. It would appear that individuals were often under geasa or solemn vows to observe, or to refrain from, certain lines of conduct – the vows being either taken on themselves voluntarily, or imposed on them, with their consent, by others. It would appear, also, that if one person went through the form of putting another under geasa to grant any reasonable request, the abjured person

> could not refuse without loss of honour and reputation.'[11]

Interesting as these comments are, they don't seem quite to cover the range and quality of all *geasa*. Was it a 'reasonable request' when Gráinne asked Diarmuid, one of Finn's faithful warriors, to marry her under Finn's nose at a wedding feast that had been arranged partly to settle an old enmity between him and her father? It's true that Diarmuid doesn't *have* to agree, but the unanimous decision of all is that though Diarmuid *may* decline Gráinne's *geasa*, he will lose all honour if he does.

Thus there seem to me to be different types of *geasa*. Gráinne's *geas* on Diarmuid is an almost insuperable injunction to do something he would never otherwise have dreamed of doing, and it involves him in loss of honour *no matter what action he takes*. The fact that he chooses to obey the *geasa* rather than keep faith with his lord shows how incredibly powerful the injunction was considered to be. (So no, not at all something you'd use to get the children to tidy up their rooms! Not something you'd use lightly.) Gráinne consented too casually to her father's wish that she become Finn's bride:

> And Grania, giving, indeed, not much thought to the matter, answered, 'I know not whether he is worthy to be thy son-in-law; but if he be, why should he not be a fitting husband for me?'[12]

---

11 Op. cit., 309.
12 Joyce, P.W., *Old Celtic Romances*, 187.

When she sees Finn, however, and realises that he is older than her father, she changes her mind. She uses the power of the *geas* as an extreme, last-minute measure, her only chance of escape.

Other *geasa* are more in the style of straightforward tabus. King Conaire must not shoot birds because his father was a bird-man, the male equivalent of the swan-maidens of many folk tales who can cast off their feathery skins and appear in human form. You don't kill the animal which is your totem, to which you are 'related' by spiritual bonds and by blood.

But the complicated *geasa* about not going righthanded (sunwise) about Tara or lefthanded (widdershins) about Bregia, or following three Reds to the House of Red, or sleeping in a house from which firelight can be seen at night, these are prophetic warnings. They are not, perhaps, quite as inescapable as the prophecies of Greek myths. When the oracle at Delphi tells Oedipus he will slay his father and marry his mother, you know it's a done deal. No matter what Oedipus does, no matter how hard he tries, *this is what will happen.* The event is more than foretold, it's ordained. In the case of Irish King Conaire, however, the *geasa* merely indicate unlucky actions which ought to be avoided: the assumption is that *some* kind of bad luck will follow the breaking of the prohibitions, but we aren't told exactly what the consequences will be. Also, the conditions laid down by the *geasa* seem arbitrary: in themselves most of them seem innocuous actions. We would all want to avoid killing our fathers and marrying our mothers. But most of us could ride clockwise around Tara, or sleep in a house with firelit windows, without coming to harm.

The *geasa* piled upon Conaire spell out a sequence of actions and omens which will lead to his death: but he cannot know this in advance. For the reader, or for the audience hearing Conaire's tale told or sung aloud, the *geasa* are a highly effective literary, poetic device for building up tension and a sense of approaching doom. In the same way, the two *geasa* laid upon Cú Chulainn – not to eat the flesh of a dog, and never to refuse an offer of food from a woman – having lain dormant for much of the tale, snap together like the jaws of a trap as the old hags call him to turn aside from his journey towards the army of Maeve to taste the meat of the hound they are cooking. It's a signal that the end is nigh. Cú Chulainn cannot escape his destiny, although the tale makes it clear that he has the opportunity – he *may* refuse, but not without dishonour, not without falling short of his own greatness. 'A great name outlasts life,' he says, like Achilles. He has already seen the Washer at the Ford:

> And presently they came to a ford, and there they saw a young girl, thin and white-skinned and having yellow hair, washing and ever washing, and wringing out clothing that was all stained crimson red, and she crying and keening all the time.
>
> 'Little Hound,' said Cathbad, 'do you see what it is that young girl is washing? It is your red clothes she is washing, and crying as she washes, because she knows you are going to your death against Maeve's great army. And take the warning now, and turn back again.'

> 'I will not turn back [said Cuchulain] . . . And what is it to me, the woman of the Sidhe to be washing red clothing for me? It is not long till there will be clothing enough, and armour and arms, lying soaked in pools of blood, by my own sword and spear. And if you are sorry and loth to let me go into the fight, I am glad and ready enough myself to go into it, though I know as well as you yourself I must fall in it. Do not be hindering me any more then,' he said, 'for, if I stay or if I go, death will meet me all the same.'[13]

I can't confidently answer the question of whether *geasa* were ever truly used in real life, outside the tales and the epics – but I would hazard a guess that they were. I'm willing to bet that there were *geasa* – prohibitions, tabus – against the killing or eating of various animals associated with ancestry and with luck, like Conaire's bird/spirit father, and Cú Chulainn's iconic struggle with the hound which gave him his name. Once Cú Chulainn had effectively *become* a hound, as he did when he offered himself to Chulainn the smith in exchange for the dog he had killed, then in a sense all dogs became his kin. Of course he could not eat them.

I'm willing also to believe there were *geasa* or prohibitions concerning all kinds of other lucky or unlucky actions or directions, because after all they still exist today: *feng shui*, not walking under ladders, not having thirteen at a dinner

13 *Cuchulain of Muirthemne*, tr. Lady Augusta Gregory, 335.

table. But the *geas* that one person could lay upon another, to compel them to do something even against their will and honour – that's something else again, and as far as I know it doesn't seem to appear in other bodies of legend. Did it ever exist? Was it a metaphor for what we now call emotional blackmail? Or was it something far more fearsome and holy, reserved perhaps for special occasions, for religio-political purposes? Was it a remnant of Druidical power?

Desiring dragons: the value of mythical thinking[1]

> Fantasy, the making or glimpsing of Other-worlds, was the heart of the desire of Faërie. I desired Dragons with a profound desire . . . [T]he world that contained even the imagination of Fafnir was richer and more beautiful, at whatever cost of peril.[2]

Myths – so runs the myth – belong to ages past, when people were naïve enough to believe in them. In modern times with our scientific explanations for the world around us, we've put away such childish things. Even children are expected to grow out of Harry Potter and fairy tales, and surely no adult found reading or writing the stuff can expect to be taken seriously?

---

1 Part of this essay was originally written in response to a question on Terri Windling's blog *Myth and Moor*: 'Why are we drawn to stories and other art forms (both contemporary and historic) with their roots dug deep in the soil of myth?'

2 Tolkien, J.R.R., 'On Fairy-Stories', *Tree and Leaf*, 40.

In a 2014 *Guardian* interview, the scientist Richard Dawkins denied having called fairy tales 'pernicious'. He admitted he had once thought 'a diet of supernatural magic spells might possibly have a detrimental effect on a child's critical thinking,' but added, 'I genuinely don't know the answer to that . . . I actually think there might be a positive benefit in fairy tales for a child's critical thinking. Do frogs turn into princes? No they don't. But an ordinary fiction story could well be true . . . So a child can learn from fairy stories how to judge plausibility.'[3]

It's kind of Dawkins to let fairy tales off from doing positive harm . . . Still, is this really the best that can be said for them? Are they to be valued only insofar as they train a child's mind to distinguish reality from fantasy, truth from lies? The ability to do so is important, yes, although more complicated than Dawkins suggests, but in any case is this really what they do? Surely fantasy, myths and legends have some intrinsic value? Surely they have something meaningful to say?

These are interesting questions. As I try to answer them in what may seem a roundabout fashion, I'll begin with an even bigger question.

What makes us human?

The answers to this one keep being refined. A special creation in the image of a God – for centuries a popular and satisfying answer? Difficult to sustain as it became clear we're just one twig on the great branching tree of evolution. Language? Perhaps, although the more we study other animals

---

3 Weaver, Matthew, 'You can call me a big bad wolf, but not a bore, says Richard Dawkins', *The Guardian*, 5 June 2014.

and birds, the more we realise that many of them communicate in quite sophisticated ways. Toolmaking? Not that distinctive, as chimpanzees and even crows employ twigs and stones as tools. An appreciation of beauty? It depends what you mean. If you think of bower-birds designing pretty nests to attract their mates, it seems clear that some animals do have an aesthetic capacity. So are we different from other animals at all?

Common sense says yes – at the very least, we have taken all these capacities incomparably further than other animals – but is it really the best we can do for a definition? At what point did our ancestors become recognisably 'us', and in what does the recognition rest?

Innovation is one answer – the development and bettering of tools. *Homo habilis* and *homo heidelbergensis* lived with one basic design of hand-axe for about a million years. When, on the other hand, we see signs of people messing about and tinkering and trying out new ideas, we recognise ourselves.

Related to this is another answer: symbolic thinking. Maybe some of our animal friends are partially capable of it – a chimpanzee can recognise a two-dimensional drawing or photograph which means nothing to a dog. But wild chimps don't indulge in representational art. Sometime, somewhere, somebody realised that lines cut in bone, or drawn in charcoal or ochre could not only make significant patterns, but could *stand for* a horse, a deer or an aurochs – an amazing leap of cognition. Beyond that, though, there had to be some fascination in the discovery, some reason to repeat it – some inherent, achieved meaning that had nothing directly to do with physical survival. What? Why?

> We are the Pilgrims, master, we shall go
> Always a little further: it may be
> Beyond the last blue mountain barred with snow,
> Across that angry or that glimmering sea,
> White on a throne or guarded in a cave
> There lives a prophet who can understand
> Why men were born . . .[4]

It may be because, somewhere along the line, human beings became sufficiently self-aware to be troubled by death. Once you truly understand that one day you're going to die, you start to look back and forth, to ask questions. *Why are we here? What was before us? Where did we come from and where will we go?*

We pass through the world surrounded by mysteries – things which *are not*, which have no physical existence. There is the past, which we remember but can no longer touch or affect: a magician's backward-facing glass in which the dead are still alive and the old are still young and can be seen going about their affairs, ignorant of our gaze, in tiny bright pictures with the sound turned down low. The physical space around us, we can touch it, yes: but then there is the distance – that blue trembling elsewhere on the rim of the horizon beyond which, perhaps, everything is different, new and wonderful. And there is the invisible future into which we constantly travel with our baggage of hopes and promises and longings and fears.

The 'mystery of existence' is an artefact. We choose to ask an answerless question, and that question is at the core of our

---

4 Flecker, James Elroy, *The Golden Journey to Samarkand*, 7.

humanity. The before-and-after of life is a great darkness and we build a bonfire to keep it out, to light and warm and comfort ourselves. The bonfire is the bonfire of culture: myths, stories, songs, music, poetry, religion, art and science. We don't need it for our physical selves; *homo heidelbergensis* got on perfectly well without it; we need it for humanity's supreme invention, the soul.

In his essay *On Fairy-Stories*, J.R.R. Tolkien considers the role of language in humanity's journey:

> [H]ow powerful, how stimulating to the very faculty that produced it was the invention of the adjective: no spell or incantation in Faerie is more potent . . . When we can take green from grass, blue from heaven and red from blood, we have already an enchanter's power . . . and the desire to wield that power in the world external to our minds awakes . . . We may put a deadly green upon a man's face and produce a horror . . . we may cause woods to spring with silver leaves and rams to wear fleeces of gold, and put hot fire into the belly of the cold worm. But in such 'fantasy' as it is called, new form is made; Faerie begins; Man becomes a sub-creator.[5]

What Tolkien called sub-creation doesn't only apply to story-tellers and artists. The Ptolemaic model of the solar system with

5 Tolkien, J.R.R., 'On Fairy-Stories', *Tree and Leaf*, 25.

the earth at its centre was believed in for centuries, and made a lot of sense given the information then available – until it was overturned by Copernicus and Galileo and Newton, and again by Einstein, and now we have string theory and branes and multiple dimensions and bubble universes; and cosmologists are continually coming up with new or refined approximations of what 'reality' may actually be (assuming the term has any meaning). This too is sub-creation. Science and religion both spring from the human struggle to apprehend the world and our place in it: and the untouchable existence of such things as the past, the future, the horizon, has given us confidence to imagine and discover and invent and delight in other things which can neither be seen nor approached nor touched. Right and wrong. Gods, ghosts and mathematics. And yes, dragons.

The modern expectation that truth should be factually based is, oddly, what religious fundamentalists and rationalists such as Richard Dawkins have in common. A fundamentalist who takes literally the Bible story of the seven days of creation refuses to accept the theory of evolution because it appears to him or her to contradict the 'facts' of the book of Genesis – not understanding that Genesis offers not factual but emotional truth, a way of accounting for our experience of the world with all its grief and joy. It is a story, a fantasy, a myth. Its purpose is not to explain the world, like a scientist. Its purpose is to reconcile us with the world.

Human beings are more complex than any single system of communication. We say some things in mathematics, some in music. Some things are best communicated physically –

comfort for a frightened child, for example. In the visual arts we express delight in form and shape and colour. The truth you get from a story is different from the truth of a proven scientific fact. The questions to ask about any work of art should be like these: *Does it move me? Has it given me something I never even knew I needed? Does it express something I always felt but didn't know how to say? Has it enriched my world?* As Karen Armstrong says, 'Any powerful work of art invades our being and changes it forever.'[6] If that happens, you will know it. It makes no sense at all to complain, 'But it's not literally true.'

So like Tolkien, I desire dragons. I long to know what lies beyond the boundaries of my five senses. I want to know what the bee sees in the ultraviolet. I want to know what it's like to hear like a bat or a dolphin. I want to know what's underneath the frozen seas of Europa, and if anything lives on Mars or on some planet circling Procyon or Alpha Centauri. I want to cross the horizon. I want to know what really happened long ago at Stonehenge and Avebury and Carnac. I want to find out what the Druids believed. And in the meantime, yes, I'll read about the golden dragons in the paradisal gardens at the end of the world because such stories are a metaphorical celebration of the magic and the miracle of 'this precious only endless world in which we think we live'.[7]

This is my credo: myths and stories deserve to be taken seriously – read and written seriously – because there are things humanity needs to say that can only be said in symbols:

---

6 Armstrong, Karen, *A Short History of Myth*, 154.

7 Graves, Robert, 'Warning to Children', Collected Poems.

The old clock ticked monotonously from the wall, the windows rattled with the whistling wind, and the chamber was dimly lighted by the flickering light of the moon. The young man lay restless on his bed, thinking of the stranger and his tales. 'It is not the treasures,' said he to himself, 'that have awakened in me such unutterable longings . . . But I long to behold the blue flower.'[8]

8 Novalis, *Henry of Ofterdingen, A Romance.*

Reflections on Single Tales

Briar Rose, or 'Time be Stopped'

Schooldays. I'm about eight years old, I have my brown school reader in my hand, and I'm about to knock on the headmistress's door. Everyone in this small school has to go and read to her once a week – a solemn ceremony and not a bad one either: there's something special about leaving the classroom while lessons are happening and making this solo pilgrimage across the quiet school hall. The door swings open and I see her room drenched in sunlight, her window opening on to a bright rose garden beyond, a garden perhaps for the teachers only, as I don't remember ever setting foot there – a secret garden. I stand beside her desk and read aloud, and the story is *Briar Rose*. And somehow the feeling of her office, this sunlit, secluded, shut-away space, weaves into the story I'm reading, so that while the tall hedge of briars springs up around the castle, and everyone, even the doves on the roof and the flies on the wall, drop into their century of sleep, I feel as though it's all happening right now, and the sleepy afternoon enfolds the school for a perfect enchanted moment, now and forever.

La Belle au bois dormant – *Briar Rose* – Sleeping Beauty – is a tale which has become almost notorious as presenting an extreme image of female passivity, the worst possible role model for a child to grow up with: a heroine who does nothing, initiates nothing, whose claim to fame is to sleep for a hundred years and be woken by the kiss of a prince she hasn't even chosen: an object rather than a subject. It's one of the most difficult fairy stories to retell, not only because the princess is passive, but because it's hard to dramatise a hundred years of nothing happening. Disney fudged the issue by simply doing away with it and introducing a fire-breathing dragon instead. His Sleeping Beauty is asleep for, at most, a few hours.

It's *Briar Rose* I want to talk about in this essay. I don't wish to get too involved in comparisons between Charles Perrault's *La Belle au bois dormant* and the Grimms' *Dornröschen*, but the two versions are very different in style, in length and in effect. Iona and Peter Opie preferred Perrault's tale (itself derived from Basile's *Pentamerone*[1]), commenting: 'it is so finely told it is no surprise that the retellings which folklorists have subsequently found in oral tradition have been flat or foolish in comparison.' They add that the Grimms' version 'possesses little of the quality of the French tale'.[2] I don't agree, although I do enjoy Perrault's light, sophisticated touch, as when he describes the Princess's clothes:

---

1 Giambattista Basile, 1575–1632. His collection of literary fairy tales, the *Pentamerone,* was published posthumously in 1636.

2 Opie, Iona and Peter, *The Classic Fairy Tales*, 102.

> She was intirely dress'd, and very magnificently, but they took care not to tell her, that she was drest like my grandmother; and had a point band peeping over a high collar . . .[3]

But it's an entertainment: there's no genuine feeling. As soon as the Princess falls asleep, the fairy whose interjection has saved her from death arrives 'in a fiery chariot drawn by dragons'. She touches with her wand every living thing in the palace, sending them individually to sleep so that they will be there when the Princess wakes – but with the exception of the King and Queen. This is so that with her parents out of the way (dead), the Princess will eventually be woken by the *new* King of the same country who, Perrault carefully explains, is 'of another family'. It's all very planned and laborious; you can hear the machinery creaking. Perrault also adds a long second half or coda in which the Princess (now Queen) is threatened by the King's ogress mother. I enjoyed it as a child, but even the Opies call it a 'seemingly unnecessary appendage' which has been 'incorrectly transmitted' from Basile. My preference now is for the organic simplicity of *Dornröschen*:

> And at the very moment when she felt the prick, she fell down upon the bed . . . and lay in a deep sleep. And this sleep extended over the whole palace . . .[4]

---

3 Opie, Iona and Peter, 'The Sleeping Beauty in the Wood,' *The Classic Fairy Tales*, 114.

4 'Little Briar Rose', KHM 50, *Grimm's Fairy Tales*, 238.

With all its bustling about and organisation, Perrault's version loses focus on what for me is the whole point of the tale, the arresting of time within the castle walls. There's beauty and terror there, the whole little jewelled world frozen and forgotten, like Pompeii under its ash, for a hundred years. (There are other tales of unearthly sleepers, like King Arthur's knights under their hill, who *still haven't woken.*) Here I find myself happily in agreement with Ursula K. Le Guin, who says very much the same thing in a fine essay, 'Wilderness Within', in her collection *Cheek by Jowl*: 'I think the story is about that still centre: "the silent house, the birdsong wilderness" . . . it is the secret garden; it is Eden; it is the dream of utter, sunlit safety; it is the changeless kingdom.'[5]

Not all stories are about people, even though they include people; not all stories are adventures. They can be about ideas, feelings, wonders – the white blink of lightning as the sky cracks and the eye of God looks through. For me this story is about the shiver you feel, which any child feels – as the storyteller says,

> The horses, too, went to sleep in the stable, the dogs in the yard, the pigeons on the roof, the flies on the wall; even the fire that was flaming on the hearth became quiet and slept, the roast meat left off frizzling, and the cook, who was just going to pull the hair of the scullery boy, because he had forgotten something, let him go and went to

5 Le Guin, Ursula K., 'Wilderness Within', *Cheek by Jowl*, 14,15.

sleep. And the wind fell, and on the trees before the castle not a leaf moved again.

But round the castle there began to grow a hedge of thorns, which every year became higher, and at last grew close up round the castle and all over it, so that there was nothing of it to be seen, not even the flag upon the roof.[6]

When you're a child, time seems endless anyway. So long to wait till your birthday! So long to wait till Christmas! The holidays stretch for ever, and even a single day at school, six short hours or so, can be an eternity of happiness or unhappiness or boredom. A hundred of anything is an enormous number. 'What would you do if you had a hundred pounds?' we used to ask one another as children. To sleep for a hundred years! The story is a meditation on Time.

T.S. Eliot's *Four Quartets* is full of the imagery of houses which rise and fall and vanish, of rose gardens and fallen petals and lost children. As it, too, is a profound meditation upon Time, am I wrong to suspect that the story of Briar Rose, the Sleeping Beauty, was somewhere in the poet's mind as he wrote?

What is Time? A cycle of recurring seasons? A river which sweeps us away? A train on a set of linear tracks, the present moment drumming ever onwards, leaving everything we have known unreachably behind? Or can Time somehow curl around us like an enclosed secret garden in which the essence

---

6 'Little Briar-Rose', KHM 50, *Grimm's Fairy Tales*, 238–9.

of everything we've loved is still real, compressed like a bowl of rose leaves, immanent, half glimpsed?

In T.F. Powys's masterpiece *Mr Weston's Good Wine*, God – in the shape of wine-salesman Mr Weston, accompanied by his angelic assistant Michael, arrives at the village of Folly Down one bleak November day in a small Ford van. Mr Weston is here to offer the villagers a choice of his wines, from the light wine of love to the dark wine of death. It's a marvellous, tender story, both comic and sad. In this passage near the middle of the book, something very odd happens in the village pub and meeting place, the Angel Inn:

> It was at this very moment – an important one in our story – following a three-minutes silence that was in itself a very strange thing in that house, that Mr Thomas Bunce happened to look at the grandfather clock. He did so because the unnatural silence that came over the company – an angel is said to be walking near when such a silence occurs – had disclosed the astonishing fact that the clock was not ticking.
>
> Mr Bunce was sure that the clock was wound. He knew that the heavy pendulum was in proper order, though no one nodded to it now; and yet the clock had stopped [...]
>
> No policeman, supposing that one of them had happened to call to see that the right and lawful hours were kept at Folly Down inn, could ever have found fault with that timepiece. The

> clock was truthful; it was even more honourable than that; it was always two minutes in advance of its prouder relation, that was set high above mankind, in the Shelton church tower.
>
> Mr Bunce stared hard at the clock. He wished to be sure.
>
> All was silent again.
>
> 'Time be stopped,' exclaimed Mr Bunce excitedly.
>
> 'And eternity have begun,' said Mr Grunter.[7]

Of course the story of *Briar Rose* continues with the prince's arrival and the blossoming of the thorns into roses, and the kiss and the awakening, because time does move and so must narratives. But the story isn't a romance. I'm sure the reason the tale has been loved for so long in spite of its quiescent heroine and miniscule plot, is all to do with that hiatus in the middle, in which nothing happens except one long moment. *Briar Rose* celebrates the gaps between the lines, the spaces between the words, the hot summer silence in the imaginary rose garden. It moves us in an almost Taoist sense to look, really *look* at the flies on the wall, the doves on the roof, the arrested gesture of the cook's hand as she slaps the serving boy – and say to ourselves, 'This – this is life.'

---

7 Powys, T.F., *Mr Weston's Good Wine*, 139.

The Juniper Tree

You cannot tell a story well unless you really love it. It's possible to fake an interest when reading aloud, because you have the support of the printed page with all its adverbs and adjectives, the author's stage directions and instructions. But put the book aside. Now try telling the story in your own words. Unless you feel a real connection with it, it will go dull and flat in a second. Storytelling must come from the heart.

Some years ago I often used to tell traditional stories to schoolchildren, and *The Juniper Tree* was one of them. 'Long ago', I would say –

> Long, long ago – more than two thousand years ago – a woman longed for a baby. Out in the courtyard of her house grew a beautiful juniper tree, and one winter day as she stood beneath it peeling an apple, she cut her finger and blood fell on the snow. 'If only I had a child as red as blood and as white as snow,' the woman sighed. And the branches of the

> juniper tree stirred as if a wind was passing through . . .'[1]

Over the next nine months, as spring comes, and summer, and the juniper tree bears fruit, the woman becomes joyfully pregnant. She eats the berries, and foresees the possibility of her death: 'If I die, bury me under the juniper tree.' She gives birth to a son and dies, and her husband buries her under the tree and grieves . . . but not for long. He marries again. His new wife bears him a daughter, little Marlinchen, and she becomes jealous of the son who will inherit the house.

So the stepmother murders the little boy. She invites him to choose an apple out of a big chest and slams down the heavy lid with its 'great, sharp lock', severing his neck. Then she tricks her daughter Marlinchen into feeling responsible. She cooks the little boy and serves him to his father in a stew, swearing Marlinchen to secrecy. Though a little troubled by his son's absence the father eats with relish, denying the food to anyone else and throwing the bones under the table. Marlinchen gathers them up in a cloth and buries them under the juniper tree – just where the child's mother was buried. A mist rises from the juniper tree, the branches stir, and out flies a beautiful fiery bird – her brother's spirit. Her sorrow vanishes and she goes comforted into the house.

The bird flies away into the village, where it sings a wonderful

---

1 My own paraphrasis.

song which tempts everyone out to listen. My version of the song ran like this:

> My mother killed her little son,
> My father grieved that I had gone.
> My gentle sister pitied me
> And buried me under the juniper tree.
> Keewit, keewit, what a happy bird I am!

I made up a haunting little tune so that I could sing these words – it didn't seem enough merely to say them. And I remember telling the story in a school hall in upstate New York to about a hundred and fifty ten-year-olds. When I reached the part about the murder, where the mother manages to unload the guilt onto her own daughter, I saw the face of a young girl sitting on the front row. Her lips had parted and her eyes were dark with horror. I did feel compunction, but the only way was to go on, telling the story to the very end – and the end is happy, one that does not negate the horror but transcends it. The burning, blazing spirit bird with its paradoxically joyful song brings delight to the innocent, terror and death to the guilty. When I'd finished, I could feel the children all relaxing. They'd followed me through a very dark place, but we'd come out into the light.

Not everyone would consider *The Juniper Tree* a suitable story for children. Was I right to tell it? I have done, many times, and no one yet has told me it was a mistake. On this occasion some of the children came up at the end and said, 'thanks for the awesome story', 'cool story!' But one of the teachers caught me and said, 'Thank you, these children don't often hear stories like that.' Over the course of the last half century fewer and fewer fairy tales have been considered appropriate for children – many have been weeded out as too strong, and the remnant has been criticised (more recently) as too insipid. Well over seventy years ago J.R.R. Tolkien complained about children being offered what he called 'mollified versions' of *The Juniper Tree* which left out the horrific details of the cannibal stew. He added, 'They should not be spared it – unless they are spared the whole story until their digestions are stronger.' In fact horror is a genre for which many children have a remarkably robust taste. *The Juniper Tree* is rooted in horror. Do away with it, and the story dies.

Without beauty, however, horror can become schlock. The tale type of *The Juniper Tree* is known as 'My Mother Killed Me, My Father Ate Me'[2]; there are many variants across Europe, often not terribly interesting. Some go in for macabre humour. In a Scots tale, *The Milk-White Doo*, the 'goodman' kills a hare and tells his wife to cook it for dinner, but the greedy wife 'aye tasted and tasted at it, till she had tasted it a' away, and then she didna ken what to do for her goodman's dinner'. Solving this minor problem in the most extreme possible way, she kills their own son Johnie and puts him in the pot. The comic effect is quite deliberate; the deadpan tone gives it away:

> Well, the goodman cam hame to his dinner, and his wife set down Johnie well boiled to him; and

---

2 Aarne-Thompson tale type 720.

when he was eating he takes up a fit [foot], and says, 'That's surely my Johnie's fit.'

'Sic nonsense! it's ane o' the hare's,' says the goodwife.

Syne he took up a hand, and says: 'That's surely my Johnie's hand.'

'You're havering, goodman; it's anither o' the hare's feet.'[3]

A story like this, told aloud, is meant to make the audience scream, laugh and shiver. *The Milk-White Doo* does the job very successfully and aims no higher. Little sister Katy gathers the child's bones and buries them under a stone by the door, where they turn into a milk white dove which flies away singing:

Pew, pew,
My minny me slew
My daddy me chew,
My sister gathered my banes
And put them between twa milk-white stanes;
And I grew, and I grew,
To a milk-white doo,
And I took to my wings, and away I flew.

'My minny me slew/My daddy me chew' – it sounds like something the storyteller would get the listening children to

3 *The Popular Rhymes of Scotland*, ed. Robert Chambers, 49.

chant: satisfying and just a little bit funny. The dove gathers gifts of clothes and silver for sister and father, and a millstone to drop on the guilty mother just as in *The Juniper Tree*; but *The Milk-White Doo* lacks the German tale's strange beauty and poignancy, and the ending is brisk:

> And it [the dove] gat the millstane; and syne it flew till it lighted on its father's house-top. It threw sma' stanes down the lum [chimney], and Katy cam out to see what the matter was; and the doo threw all the claes [clothes] to her. Syne the father cam out, and the doo threw a' the siller to him. And syne the mother cam out, and the doo threw down the millstane upon her and killed her. And at last it flew away; and the goodman and his dochter after that
>
> Lived happy, and died happy,
> And never drank out of a dry cappy.[4]

'And then this . . . and then this . . . and then that . . .' It's very serial. There's no emotion, no anticipation, no sense of gathering catastrophe. Much of the effect of this story, which the editor Robert Chambers tells us was 'familiar in every Scottish nursery fifty years ago' (i.e., circa 1820) is left to the energy of the storyteller and the participation of the listeners.

---

4 Op. cit., 50.

Another version is a Devonshire tale, *The Rose-Tree*, first recorded in 1866 and republished by Joseph Jacobs in *English Fairy Tales*. A jealous stepmother sends her pretty stepdaughter to the grocer's to buy a pound of candles, but on the way home the child puts the candles down to climb over a stile. 'Up came a dog and ran off with the candles.' After three repetitions of the event the child goes home crying, having spent all the money. This opening doesn't seem to belong with the rest of the tale and feels strangely irrelevant, but the loss of the candles angers the stepmother. Pretending to comb and part the little girl's golden hair, she strikes off the child's head with an axe and cooks heart and liver for her husband's dinner, but her little son refuses to eat.

> He ran out into the garden, and took up his little sister, and put her in a box, and buried the box under a rose-tree; and every day he went to the tree and wept, till his tears ran down on the box.

One day, the rose tree flowered. It was spring, and there among the flowers was a white bird, and it sang, and sang, and sang like an angel out of heaven. Away it flew, and it went to a cobbler's shop, and perched itself on a tree hard by; and thus it sang:

> 'My wicked mother slew me
> My dear father ate me,
> My little brother whom I love

> Sits below, and I sing above.
> Stick, stock, stone dead.'[5]

The story then follows the traditional pattern. The dove collects red shoes from the cobbler, a gold watch from the jeweller and a millstone from the miller. It flies back to the house and rattles the millstone against the eaves of the house with a sound like thunder.

> Then the little boy ran out to see the thunder, and down dropped the red shoes at his feet. [The dove] rattled the millstone against the eaves of the house once more, and the stepmother said again, 'It thunders.' Then the father ran out and down fell the chain about his neck. In ran father and son, laughing and saying, 'See what the thunder has brought us!'[6]

The stepmother thinks the thunder will bring something for her. She steps outside, and down falls the millstone upon her head. In neither *The Milk-White Doo* nor *The Rose-Tree* is the murdered child restored to life.

The Juniper Tree is a more literary and much greater rendering of this traditional tale. The brothers Grimm did not collect it themselves. They used a Low German[7] dialect version

---

5 Jacobs, Joseph, *English Fairy Tales*, 17.
6 Op. cit., 19.
7 *Plattdeutsch*, once spoken over an area extending from the north-

published in 1808 by the Romantic poet and artist Philipp Otto Runge, who almost certainly rewrote and extended his oral source. Unlike other variants his opening paragraphs focus on the woman's longing for a child, establishing at once a mystical communion between her and the juniper tree. The moment when her blood falls on the snow beneath the juniper 'is' the moment of conception, and as if to emphasise this, her child's development in the womb imitates or is imitated by external nature. Maria Tatar comments, '[Runge's] is the only extant version of the tale which weds the biological mother so closely to nature – once she becomes fertile and conceives, she is turned into a virtual prisoner of nature, subject to its laws of growth and decay.'[8]

This is not quite what I draw from the plangent beauty of the opening.

> [A] month went by and the snow was gone, and two months, and then everything was green, and three months, and then all the flowers came out of the earth, and four months, and then all the trees in the wood grew thicker, and the green branches were all closely entwined, and the birds sang until the wood resounded and the blossoms fell from the trees, then the fifth month passed and she stood under the juniper tree, which smelt so sweetly that her heart leapt, and she fell on her

east Netherlands through northern Germany and into Poland.

8 Tatar, Maria, *Off With Their Heads!*, 220.

> knees and was beside herself with joy, and when the sixth month was over the fruit was large and fine, and then she was quite still, and the seventh month she snatched at the juniper berries and ate them greedily, then she grew sick and sorrowful, then the eighth month passed, and she called her husband and wept and said, 'If I die, then bury me under the juniper tree.' Then she was quite comforted and happy until the next month was over, and then she had a child as white as snow and as red as blood, and when she beheld it she was so delighted that she died.[9]

I take issue with Tatar's word 'prisoner', which implies a loss of agency. Prisoners are constrained, confined, unwilling. By becoming pregnant the woman has indeed subjected herself to an inevitable natural process which may end in her death, but it is a state she has literally willed and longed for, and its proper outcome is new life. The passage is a moving account of the woman's different emotions as she looks ahead to childbirth – now in tears, now hopeful, peaceful, ecstatic, now sick and sorrowful, now content. She dies in an excess of delight, and the ebb and flow of emotion continues through the tale as little Marlinchen too fluctuates between bitter grief, mysterious content and inexplicable joy.

For a fairy tale, *The Juniper Tree* pays minute and unusual attention to shadings of emotion among its characters, tracing

---

9 'The Juniper Tree', KHM 47, *Grimm's Fairy Tales*, 221.

the significance of individual responses to the same events. When the goldsmith, shoemaker and miller's men hear the song of the miraculous bird, they stop work, run outside, exclaim. The shoemaker calls out to his wife:

> 'Wife, just come outside, there is a bird, look at that bird, he certainly can sing!' Then he called his daughter and children, and apprentices, boys and girls, and they all came up the street and looked at the bird and saw how beautiful he was, and what fine red and green feathers he had, and how like real gold his neck was, and how the eyes in his head shone like stars. 'Bird,' said the shoemaker, 'now sing me that song again.'

It may seem a strange response to a song which catalogues such dreadful deeds. Why are these people not struck with horror? It's because this is a fairy tale and they are innocent, so the accusatory words do not affect them – literally mean nothing; it's as if they do not hear them. They respond only to the song's beauty. Each time it sings, the bird/child/spirit ends with an exclamation of deep personal delight. It cannot be hurt any more. It is strong and beautiful, beyond death and sorrow, and is bringing healing and justice.

> My mother she killed me
> My father he ate me,
> My sister, little Marlinchen,
> Gathered together all my bones,

Tied them in a silken handkerchief,
Laid them beneath the juniper tree.
Kywitt, kywitt, what a beautiful bird am I![10]

When the bird flies back to its father's house and sits on the roof, the father feels happy in much the same way as the townsfolk, but with a more personal connection: 'as if I were about to see some old friend again'. Like the townsfolk he does not take in the meaning of the words because he, too, is innocent: he does not know he has eaten his son's flesh; he does not know the child is dead. Only the stepmother and Marlinchen are complicit in this terrible knowledge. The song strikes home to both of them, but their responses are different. Where the stepmother feels unease and dread, Marlinchen is overcome with grief. As the bird repeats his song, the stepmother becomes increasingly terrified, while Marlinchen lays her head on her knees and sobs harder. The father, however, feels an increasing sense of wellbeing. 'The sun shines so warm and there's a smell like cinnamon!' He goes outside and the bird tosses a golden chain around his neck. As it begins the song again, the stepmother tries to stop her ears, crying, 'Would that I were a thousand feet beneath the earth so as not to hear that!' But heartened by the bird's gift to her father, Marlinchen goes out and it throws down the gift of red shoes to her, as if in forgiveness and blessing.

Marlinchen needs forgiveness because although she is innocent, she feels guilty. Not knowing that his neck was

---

10 'The Juniper Tree', KHM 47, *Grimm's Fairy Tales*, 224.

already severed, she thinks she killed her brother by boxing his ears and knocking off his head. Her mother has tricked her and then manipulated her into concealing what happened: 'What have you done? Keep quiet and let no one know. There's nothing to be done about it now; we will cook him in a stew.' Marlinchen is her mother's second victim, and the creepy message *it's your fault and you must never tell* is something the tale clearly recognises as child abuse. Now the gift of the bird/brother/spirit absolves Marlinchen. She dances back into the house, healed. 'I was so sad when I went out, and now I am so light-hearted!'

> 'Well,' said the woman, and sprang to her feet and her hair stood up like flames of fire, 'I feel as if the world were coming to an end! I too will go out and see if my heart feels lighter.' And as she went out at the door, crash! the bird threw down the millstone upon her head, and she was entirely crushed by it.[11]

Flames, smoke and fire rise from the spot and when it clears, the little brother stands there alive again, 'and he took his father and Marlinchen by the hand and all three were right glad, and they went into the house to dinner, and ate.'

Why a juniper tree? Whether the tree is in fact a juniper depends on the meaning of the Low German word *Machandelboom*. Even the brothers Grimm weren't entirely

11 'The Juniper Tree', KHM 47, *Grimm's Fairy Tales*, 229.

sure. They felt the closest approximation was '*mandelbaum*' or 'almond tree', but suggested in their notes the tree could instead be a '*wacholderbaum*', a juniper. Most though not all English translators seem to have gone for this option, although the fruit of the juniper (not even a berry, actually a tiny modified cone) isn't really something that grows 'large and fine', nor is it something one can easily imagine a pregnant woman desiring.

Has the juniper anything to do with children or fertility? In his *Teutonic Mythology* Jacob Grimm refers briefly to an Indian belief that the juniper is the 'Tree of Wishes', and quotes a rhyme from another fairy tale in which a woman reproaches Frau Weckoller, the spirit of the juniper, for stealing her child.[12] Alexander Porteus seems to support this when he speaks of Frau Wachholder (Dame Juniper) 'the genius of the Juniper tree' who can be called upon to make thieves to give back their booty, and mentions that in north-west India the tree *Juniperus excelsus* 'was the abode of a Tree Spirit which caused women to bear children and flocks to multiply'.[13] Finally, a legend widely disseminated on the internet but which I am unable to source names a juniper tree as sheltering the Holy Family on the Flight into Egypt.[14]

Is there any other connection? In *The Life of Heinrich Stilling*, a fictionalised autobiography published in 1777, there's a ballad in which a juniper tree, and a bird which flies

---

12 Grimm, Jacob, *Teutonic Mythology*, Vol II, 652.

13 Porteus, Alexander, *The Lore of the Forest*, 93 and 168.

14 Several online platforms erroneously state that this legend can be found in one of the Apocryphal Infancy Gospels, specifically the Syriac/Arabic. I have checked and it is in none of them.

away with a golden ring, are associated with the final parting of two siblings, a knight and his sister. As they bid each other farewell, the sister sings:

> Ich sah, mein schonstes Brüderlein
> Ein buntig, artig Vögelein
> Es hüpfte in Wacholderbaum.
> Ich warfe mit meinem Ringelein
> Es nahm ihn in sein Schnabelein
> Und flog weg in dem Walde fort
> Kein Ringelein war ewig fort
> Adie! Adie! Adie![15]

> My dearest brother, I once did see –
> As it hopped about in the juniper tree –
> A beautiful bird with plumage gay:
> I threw my ring at it in a freak
> It caught it up in its little beak
> And flew into the forest far away.
> Adieu, adieu, adieu. [16]

So is a *Machandelboom* a juniper or not? Probably yes, but it may not matter much. The species of the tree differs in any case from tale to tale. The English variant is a rose tree, and in *The Milk-White Doo* there is no tree at all. More significant is that *The Juniper Tree*'s identification of the boy's natural

---

15 Jung, Johann Heinrich, *Heinrich Stillings Jugend*, 29.
16 Jung, Johann Heinrich, *The Autobiography of Heinrich Stilling*, 7.

mother, in life and in death, with the tree at whose roots she is actually buried, is reminiscent of the magical hazel tree which Aschenputtel plants on her mother's grave. In that tale, too, a bird-spirit appears in the branches to throw down gifts (silver and gold dresses) to her deserving child. Trees are alive, that's the point, and they harbour birds which can fly up to heaven. In the New Testament the Holy Spirit descends in the form of a dove, and the phoenix – which the colourful bird in *The Juniper Tree* resembles – is an emblem of resurrection.

So what does *The Juniper Tree* mean? It depends whom you ask and when you ask them. Maria Tatar, who devotes a whole, thoughtful chapter to the tale in her book *Off With their Heads!*, suggests that the tale 'can be read as a story responding to the distress felt by a child growing up under the weight of guilt (whether consciously registered or not) produced by the death of a mother during childbirth.' She concludes,

> The version of The Juniper Tree in the Grimms' *Nursery and Household Tales* may in the past have proved therapeutic to children who felt that they had murdered their mothers (literally or symbolically), and it may well still serve that function today. But this tale, like so many tales of family life, also serves the more general purpose of empowering children, or at least making children feel less inferior to adults. In cultures that consistently place adult authority

> against childish impotence and inadequacy, these stories have a liberating power that should not be underestimated.[17]

This is an interesting and valid interpretation, but it is of course an intellectual, critical response, not an instinctive and primary one. Tatar offers *an* interpretation, not *the* interpretation. She knows that fairy tales are texts capable, probably, of as many interpretations as they have readers. What does it mean, to say *this is what something means*? What happens when you read or listen to *The Juniper Tree*; what happens to *you*? For J.R.R. Tolkien:

> [T]he chief flavour of that tale lingering in the memory was not beauty or horror, but distance and a great abyss of time, not measurable even by *twe tusend Johr.* Without the stew and the bones . . . that vision would largely have been lost. I do not think I was harmed by the horror *in the fairy-tale setting*, out of whatever dark beliefs and practices of the past it may have come. Such stories . . . open a door on Other Time, and if we pass through, if only for a moment, we stand outside our own time, outside Time itself, maybe.[18]

---

17 Tatar, Maria, *Off With Their Heads!*, 223–6.
18 Tolkien, J.R.R., 'On Fairy Tales,' *Tree and Leaf*, 32–3.

Though this too is not my own take on the tale, I acknowledge its power; if Tolkien's response means more to me than Tatar's – it does – this is because however interesting the search for meanings may be, what comes first is the story's 'flavour', the burst of juice on the tongue, the almost physical interaction between us and it. The emotional effect is primary. You can work out why it happens – if you can – afterwards.

So I can't tell you what *The Juniper Tree* means, only what it means to me. It's a strong story, full of joy and pain. It packs a lot into a little space. It's about longing and loss and grief, fulfilment and joy. It's about those rare days when the sun shines and the air smells sweet as cinnamon, and life is good. It's about jealousy, cruelty and abuse. It's about the power of nature, beauty and music. It's about revenge, justice and restitution. It acknowledges terrible evil, but it ends in hope. Like a poem, it says different things to different people at different times. It isn't something you can uncork like a bottle and extract the scribbled message within. It's itself. It's *The Juniper Tree*. It haunts me.

The King Who had Twelve Sons

This story, which is where I first read and fell in love with the phrase 'seven miles of steel thistles', is not exactly well known. I found it in a lovely but shabby old book I picked up in a second-hand bookshop. Old books have personalities and so I shall describe it: spine bound in red cloth with gilt lettering, boards covered in green cloth with a gilt medallion on the front cover, pages a little drunken and furry-edged, stitching loose. It is *West Irish Folk-Tales and Romances*, collected and translated by William Larminie ('*with introduction and notes, and appendix containing specimens of the Gaelic originals phonetically spelt*'). It was published by the Camden Library in 1893, and was reviewed and praised by William Butler Yeats who wrote:

> These little stories of Mr Larminie's have no moral, and yet, perhaps, they and their like are the only things really immortal, for they were told in some shape or other, by old men at the fire before Nebuchadnezzar ate grass, and they will still linger in some odd crannie or crevice

> of the world when the pyramids have crumbled into sand. Their appeal is to the heart and not the intellect. They take out emotions and fashion them into forms of beauty, as a goldsmith fashions gold . . .[1]

William Larminie was born in County Mayo in 1849 and died in 1900. He was a minor Irish poet and a folklorist. He spoke Gaelic, and translated most of the stories in the book from named oral storytellers:

> All have been taken down in the same way – that is to say, word for word from the dictation of peasant narrators . . . difficult and doubtful parts being gone over again and again. Sometimes the narrator can explain difficulties. Sometimes other natives of the place can help you. But after every resource of this kind has been exhausted, a certain number of doubtful words and phrases remain, with regard to which – well, one can only do one's best.

Though Yeats unthinkingly refers to the stories as 'Mr Larminie's', Larminie himself takes care to credit his narrators, going into some detail about who they are and where they come from. This is really fascinating:

---

1 Yeats, William Butler, 'The Evangel of Folk-lore', *Writings on Irish Folklore, Legend and Myth*, 136.

> Renvyle . . . is situated in Connemara . . . Terence Davis is a labourer pure and simple. A man of about forty-five years of age, and blind in one eye. Some of his tales he got from his mother . . .
>
> Next in order, Achill Island, some twenty five miles from Renvyle by sea, more than sixty miles by land. Two narrators from that locality are . . . represented in the book. One of them, Pat. McGrale, is a man of middle age, a cottier with a small holding and besides, a Jack-of-all-trades, something of a boatman and fisherman, 'a botch of a tailor', to use his own words, and ready for any odd job. He can read Irish, but had very little literature on which to exercise his accomplishment. He knows some long poems by heart, and is possessed of various odds and ends of learning, accurate and not. John McGinty, a man of Donegal descent and name, has also some land; but his holding is so small that he is to a great extent a labourer for others, and was engaged on relief works when I first came to know him. He, also, is a middle aged man. He knows many Ossianic poems by heart, which, he told me, his father taught him, verse by verse . . .

It is John McGinty who told William Larminie the tale of *The King Who Had Twelve Sons*. I've never read a story which provides a better simulation of actually being there and listening to the story-teller: it's picaresque, free-moving, and full of minor inconsistencies; so you have to keep your wits about you and hang on to your hat. I'd like to share my experience of it. This is how it starts:

> He went down to the river every day and killed a salmon for each one of them.[2]

Who did? Who is this? Who's 'them'? What's happening? Ah, this is what the King who had twelve sons did, of course! We've been flung into the middle of a conversation here. John (Séan?) McGinty has already introduced the story by its title and plunged straight in.

> He saw a duck on the river and twelve young birds with her; and she was beating the twelfth away from her. He went to the old druid and asked what was the cause why the duck was beating the twelfth bird from her. 'It was this,' said the old druid, 'she gave the bird to God and the Djachwi.'

The King immediately decides to do the same thing as the duck:

> The younger children were running on first to the

---

2 'The King Who had Twelve Sons', *West Irish Folk-Tales*, ed. William Larminie, 196 et seq.

> house, being hungry, and the eldest was coming, reading a book, after them. The father was standing at the gate on the inside, and he threw him a purse of money and told him he must go seek his fortune, that he gave him to God and the Djachwi.

When I first read this, I had no idea what the Djachwi might be. The story never tells, and the relevant note by Larminie at the back of the book, which presumably ventured a guess, had been torn away. I later learned from a fascinating article by Monika Kropej that the term stems from the Old Irish word for ten or tenth and refers to a legend that the tenth child (or in some cases the seventh or twelfth) must roam the world as either a sacrifice to, or a personification of, Fate or Destiny.[3] In any case, the Djachwi never re-enters the story. This is merely the kick-start to get the son away from the house and on the road to adventure. Note that the King is no grander than any small crofter or farmer, with a garden and a garden gate . . .

The son gets up early next morning, 'washed his face and prayed to God' and gives the druid a 'good heap' of gold. In return the druid gives him a bridle. Off goes the son and takes service with another king he meets on the road. As wages he demands 'the beast that comes and puts his head in this bridle mine.' A couple of days later he hears great news:

---

3 Kropej, Monika, 'The Tenth Child in Folk Tradition', *Studia Mythologica Slavica* 3, 75–88.

> 'The daughter of the King of the great Wren is to be devoured tomorrow by a piast.'

Here a footnote explains that a piast is '*a Gaelic monster, not exactly equivalent to either serpent or dragon.*' There's no explanation about the Wren, though, and the lad's informant continues with great and realistic unconcern:

> 'Was it in a wood or a hole in the ground you've been, that you didn't hear it? Gentle and simple of the three islands are to be there tomorrow to look at the piast swallowing her – at twelve o' clock tomorrow.'

Naturally, the lad goes riding off to save her.

> He called for his second best suit of clothes, and it came to him with a leap; and he shook the bridle, and the ugliest pony in the stables came to him and put her head in the bridle. 'Be up riding on me with a jump' (said the pony) lowering himself on his two knees. He gave his face to the way and he would overtake the wind of March that was before him, and the wind of March that was after would not overtake him. When he came in sight of the place where the gathering was, the piast was coming till she was half upon the land; and he and the piast went fighting, till he tore her with his mouth and feet.

You wouldn't notice in the excitement of the telling, perhaps, but the pony changes between two sentences from 'her' to 'him' and it may not be immediately obvious, but the 'he' in the second half of this paragraph is not the lad but the pony. It's the pony, not the boy that kills the piast! The princess is saved and, in a Cinderella-like motif, she pulls off the lad's boot as he rides by. 'She proclaimed a gathering of all the men in the three islands, that she might see who the man was that the shoe fitted.' The lad turns up and,

> She knew him at once. The shoe was in her hand and it leaped from her hand till it went on his foot. "You are the man that was on the pony on the day that he killed the piast, and you are the man whom I will marry."

It's nice to encounter a princess so decisive and authoritative. The pair marry and 'spent that night part in talking and part in storytelling'. It sounds an idyllic union; but the very next day the lad finds 'an apple of gold' upon the beach. The pony tells him not to pick it up – it will bring him trouble – but the lad ignores the pony's advice. 'He went home, and the pearl of gold with him,' and the old druid (remember him?) tells him it belongs to 'the daughter of a king of the eastern world, who lost it from her hair; – that there was a pearl of gold on every rib of her hair'.

And now the lad wants to find her.

> The pony told him that she was hard to see. 'There

> are seven miles of hill on fire to cross before you come to where she is, and there are seven miles of steel thistles, and seven miles of sea for you to go over. I told you to have nothing to do with the apple.'

Right . . . so the apple of gold has morphed into a pearl in the space of two sentences, and the lad is getting conflicting advice from druid and pony. We have come a long way from the boy's father, the eponymous King Who Had Twelve Sons: we've had three kings already and are about to meet a fourth, while the boy is about to collect a second princess. He rides over the seven miles of hill on fire, the seven miles of steel thistles and the seven miles of sea. He leaps the pony into the castle where she lives, catches her up and leaps out with her, and takes her home. '"Now," said the pony, "strike your rod of druidism upon me, and make of me a rock of stone."' The pony is turned into a rock, which can become a pony once again if struck with this 'rod of druidism' which we didn't know the boy had.

So now there are two women in the castle.

> And the young queen he married did not know . . . till the hen-wife told her. 'Well!' said the hen-wife. 'He has no regard for you beside the other. There is an apple of gold on every rib of hair upon her head.'

Where on earth did the hen-wife spring from? Oh well, I suppose every castle has one; and on her advice the young queen plays cards with the lad till he loses. For a forfeit she commands him to bring her 'the black horse of the bank'. (Could this be a kelpie, a water horse? There's no knowing.) The lad strikes the rock and brings the pony back to life, and the pony fights the black horse and brings it home.

At this point, I don't know about you, but I'm on the side of the young queen who was rescued from the piast. I'm expecting this to be her story now. And so it is for a while. She and her husband continue to play cards and send each other on tit-for-tat errands. The queen has to fetch 'the three black ravens that are in the eastern world' and succeeds, helped by friendly giants: but – feeling contrary no doubt, and who would blame her? – releases them, once her husband has seen them:

> 'If I promised to bring them to you, I did not promise to give them to you.'

Now, however, the young man gets irritated by the hen-wife's interference. He summons her and sends her off to find 'the Gruagach[4] of the Apple, and bring . . . the sword of light that is with the King of Rye'.

Are you still with me? Still keeping up with the storyteller John McGinty as he leaps from character to character – from King to lad, from lad to queen, from queen to hen-wife – agile as a man crossing a river on stepping stones?

The hen-wife succeeds in her task with the help of a friendly

---

4 'In old Gaelic, 'Gruagach' meant a young chief, or more literally 'the long-haired one', but later it came to be used of a spirit': Jane C. Beck, 'The White Lady of Great Britain and Ireland', 302.

smith (at the cost of losing the tips of both her little fingers) and brings back the sword of light with, additionally, the King of Rye's 'divided stone of druidism' – both of which the smith begs the hen-wife to return before the King puts him to death.

Now then! Surely it's time for this story to spring back on itself and wrap everything up neatly at last! But what do we get? A row of asterisks:

* * * * * *

And a footnote:

> *The narrator's memory failed him at this point, and he was unable to relate the further developments of this remarkable game of plot and counterplot. Although the hen-wife was successful in the last event mentioned, it must be inferred that she was ultimately defeated.*

So we never find out anything more about the Gruagach of the Apple, or whether the hen-wife gets back to the smith, or if the pony had anything more to say . . . All John McGinty could remember of the rest of the story was its last, disconnected and downbeat sentence:

> And when the first wife saw the second wife with her own eyes, she could esteem herself no longer, and she died of a broken heart.

Here are some asterisks of my own:

* * * * * *

Now why have I spent so much time telling you about this story when John McGinty himself couldn't remember what happened? What's the good of a story (as Alice might say) with no proper ending?

For me, the good of it is that it demonstrates the process by which all fairy tales have come down to us. There are many oral storytellers today, as there are many folk and ballad singers – and I've tried my hand at both – but most of the time, the way most of us encounter fairy stories and folk tales is by reading them in books. And fairy tales in books are like fossils, or Sleeping Beauty's castle, preserved in time and growing more and more dated. Fairy tales on the printed page are finished, unchanging, canonical, anonymous. Fairy tales told aloud are fuzzy-edged, fluid, variable – and belong to the person who is telling them, *for so long as they are upon his or her tongue.*

I'm impressed by the honesty which led William Larminie to include this incomplete story in his collection. It starts promisingly, it has many intriguing developments – but in the end, we don't know what happens. We never will know. John McGinty forgot.

Although perhaps, a week or two later on another night, stung by his failure to tell the story all the way through, John McGinty did remember the whole thing, but Larminie wasn't there. Or perhaps, McGinty strung on to it the ending of some other story, which could be appropriately altered to fit. Or perhaps he made something up out of his own head. That's the way storytelling works. It isn't fixed, it isn't canonical. This broken telling is 'authentic'.

If I added an ending of my own, it wouldn't be authentic at all.

Or would it?

'This story is true,' as one of the other tales in the book concludes. 'All the other ones are lies.'

The Great Silkie of Sule Skerry

An eart'ly nourris sits and sings,
And aye she sings 'Ba lily wean;
'Little ken I my bairnis father,
Far less the land that he staps in.'

So begins the old ballad of *The Great Silkie of Sule Skerry*, first collected by Lieutenant F.W.L. Thomas R.N., in 1852. As he explains,

> I wrote down the following ballad from the dictation of a venerable lady-udaller,[1] who lived at Snarra Voe, a secluded district in Shetland. The story is founded on the superstition of the Seals or Selkies being able to throw off their waterproof jackets, and assume the more graceful proportions of the genus Homo . . . Silky is a common name

1 'Udaller': a land-holder under the non-feudal, unwritten udal system then common in the Northern Isles.

> in the north country for a seal, and appears to be a corruption of *selch*, the Norse word for that animal. Sule Skerry is a small rocky islet, lying about twenty-five miles to the westward of Hoy Head, in Orkney, from whence it may be seen in very clear weather . . .[2]

We shall come back to the rather charming Lieutenant Thomas in a moment, but to expand upon his words: although the selkie of this particular ballad is a male, the best-known selkie tales involve a seal woman captured or taken to wife by a mortal man, usually a fisherman, who spies her in mortal form dancing on a moonlit beach and steals her discarded skin, preventing her from changing back into a seal. Such stories generally end when the selkie bride discovers her hidden sealskin and returns to the sea, leaving her mortal husband and children to mourn. With their powerful emotional charge, selkie tales have attracted a number of modern treatments including the impressive *Sea Hearts*[3] by Australian writer Margo Lanagan in which the men of Rollrock Island reject their human wives in favour of beautiful, passive selkie brides. In my own *Troll Mill* (second part of the trilogy *West of the Moon*)[4] I found in the selkie's return to the sea, abandoning her child, a metaphor for postnatal depression. Emerging from these tales are themes of power and powerlessness in sexual relationships,

---

2 *Proceedings of the Society of Antiquaries of Scotland, Vol 1*, 86.

3 Lanagan, Margo, *Sea Hearts*, published in US & UK as *The Brides of Rollrock Island.*

4 Langrish, Katherine, *West of the Moon*, 173–4.

of love, longing and loss; and *The Great Selkie of Sule Skerry* is no exception. Stories about selkies are ambiguous, evocative, sad.

Probably this is in part because of the way seals themselves affect our emotions. Bobbing curiously up around boats, they seem to show as much interest in us as we in them, and there is something mysteriously human about their faces and their mournful cries. In his introduction to the ballad Lieutenant Thomas gives a vivid account of the seals at home in their own kingdom:

> There is usually among a herd of seals, one individual whose bulk, age and scars, identify him as the patriarch of his tribe, in fact, the 'Great Silkie' . . . One of their breeding places is at the Ve (sacred) Skerries, situate upon the west side of Shetland, several miles from the land. These rocks are almost covered by the sea at high water, and, in this stormy climate, a heavy surf breaking over them, generally forms an effectual barrier to boats. It was once my fortune, after having passed the night at the Haaf-fishing (for cod, ling etc) to fall in with these rocks when pulling for the land. The morning was very foggy, but there was no wind, and the sea was as smooth as a mirror. We pulled for nearly a mile through the narrow channels formed by a thousand weed-covered skerries, upon which the monsters of the deep were reposing, and as we passed they leisurely

> raised their heads to look curiously at the strangers; a few rolled themselves into the water and swam after us, but most remained on shore to guard their young. The mist shrouded us so completely, that we caused no general alarm, and nursing operations continued undisturbed. But the lullaby was anything but euphonious, for . . . near us, but unseen, some Phocine[5] monster would give utterance to a roar, such as only could be imagined from the throat of Cerberus; then groans and sighs expressive of unutterable torment, were followed by a melancholy howl of hopeless despair . . . and for miles and more the bellow of the sea-monsters resounded through the still and heavy air.[6]

I too have heard the seals singing. Last year, wandering on the fractured rocky shore of Longstone Island off the coast of Northumberland, I became aware of an eerie sound in the air. Keening, moaning, huff-huff-huffing – hooting like children who make long quavering ghost noises – a group of seals, more than twenty of them, were crying to one another as they lay on a ridge at the edge of the tide. *Whoooo!*

There are several different versions of *The Great Silkie of Sule Skerry*, and I'll look in detail at some of the others later, but let's stick for now with Lieutenant Thomas and the one he

---

5 Phocine: of or relating to seals, from Latin *phōca*, a seal.
6 *Proceedings of the Society of Antiquaries of Scotland, Vol 1*, 87.

collected from the old lady of Snarra Voe. (It also happens to be the earliest.)

The ballad opens with an 'earthly nourrice' – that is, a mortal woman nursing her child – lamenting that she doesn't know who his father is:

> 'Little ken I my bairnis father,
> Far less the land that he staps in.[7]

What does it mean, that the woman doesn't know who her child's father is? How can that happen? It could happen if she's been promiscuous, but it could also happen if she has been raped. Rape occurs a lot in ballads, much of it quite casual, probably reflecting everyday life. So here's this woman, this unnamed woman, rocking and nursing her child, not knowing who his father is (and therefore unsupported, vulnerable): and something fearful happens.

> Then ane arose at her bed fit
> An' a grumly guest I'm sure was he;
> 'Here am I thy bairn's father,
> Although that I be not comelie.

'One arose at her bed foot' – in her home, her bower, into the safe place where she's nursing her child, there emerges, surges up like an apparition from the foot of the bed, this grim, rough creature which – perhaps – once forced itself upon her. And he acknowl-

7 'Staps': stops, dwells.

edges her child as his. And he tells her the terrible truth: he's not even human, and if he has a home at all other than the wild sea, it's only a tiny rock far out in the North Atlantic, far from land.

> 'I am a man upo' the lan'
> An' I am a Silkie in the sea;
> And when I'm far and far frae lan'
> My dwelling is in Sule Skerrie.'

The woman reproaches him.

> 'It was na weel,' quo the maiden fair,
> 'It was na weel, indeed,' quo' she;
> 'That the great Silkie of Sule Skerry
> S'uld hae come and aught[8] a bairn to me.'

This is how the selkie responds.

> Now he has ta'en a purse of goud,
> And he has pat it upo' her knee
> Sayin' 'Gie to me my little young son,
> An' tak thee up thy nourris fee.'

My first reaction is that he's paying her off, flinging money into her lap, treating her like a hireling. 'Pick up your money and give me my son.' All the authority, all the power is on the selkie father's side. His indifference is chilling, ruthless. But would it

---

8 'Aught': owned.

have seemed so to the ballad's first audience? Or would they rather have felt that in acknowledging his son, and giving gold to the woman, the selkie is acting responsibly? It may be so, for the next verse is delectably tender. One hot summer day, the selkie will take his little half-mortal son and teach him how to 'swim the foam':

> 'An' it sall come to pass on a simmer's day,
> Quehn the sin shines het on evera stane;
> That I will tak my little young son
> An' teach him how to swim the faem.'

But then it will all go wrong. In the last verse, the selkie, as a supernatural creature, foresees the end.

> 'An thu sall marry a proud gunner,
> An' a proud gunner I'm sure he'll be;
> An' the very first schot that ere he schoots,
> He'll schoot baith my young son and me.'

What's the point then – if it was always going to end in such tragedy? Why did the selkie take the woman in the first place, why did he father her child? You might as well ask, 'What is the point of *Hamlet*?' The ballad is a song, a poem, and if it's about anything it's about the harshness and unfairness of the world, and the brevity and beauty of life. The best moments are in the last-but-one verse: it's full of light: the glorious heat of the sun on the shoreline stones in the short, bright northern summer, and the sensuous joy of the bond between the selkie and his 'little young son' as he teaches him to swim. Those are the moments that make the story bearable – and surely, the ballad suggests, those are the moments which make human life bearable, however brief it may be.

These were my thoughts when I wrote about this ballad for the first time, and posted the piece on my blog back in March 2014. Coming to it afresh for this collection, I picked up my copy of *The Oxford Book of Ballads* to refresh my memory, turned to the right page – and blinked. The title was different:[9] *The Grey Selchie of Sule Skerry*. The first verse was different, too.

> In Norway land there lived a maid,
> Hush ba loo lillie, this maid began:
> I know not where my baby's father is,
> Whether by land or sea does he travel in.

This wasn't at all how I remembered it! In comes 'a good grey selchie' who announces that he is the baby's father and his name is 'good Hein Mailer', adding:

> I am a man upon the land,
> I am a selchie in the sea,
> And whin I'm far from every strand
> My dwelling is [on] Shool Skerry.

This core verse was more or less unchanged, but the details and

---

9 'The Grey Selchie of Sule Skerry', *The Oxford Book of Ballads*, ed. James Kinsley, 91.

wording of nearly all the other lines were strange to me. The ballad was longer, too, and had changed character: less intense but more comprehensible, more of a story. I didn't like it so much.

I knew I had first come across *The Great Silkie of Sule Skerry* in *The Oxford Book of Ballads* – but in Arthur Quiller Couch's edition of 1910. I looked at the volume I was holding. It was James Kinsley's 1969 edition, with a new and very different selection of ballads. He had replaced *The Great Silkie* with *The Grey Selchie.* But why? And where had *The Grey Selchie* come from? My curiosity was piqued, I wanted to know more. I set about trying to trace the history of the various different versions of the ballad.

The first and oldest printed version we have is *The Great Silkie*, which the anonymous old lady at Snarra Voe, Shetland, sang to Lieutenant Thomas[10] no later than 1852, the year he published it in *Proceedings of the Society of Scottish Antiquaries.* There it sat for three decades until in 1885 Francis James Child republished it in his monumental *English and Scottish Popular Ballads* (where it gained the tag 'Child 113'). Last in the sequence, in 1910 Arthur Quiller-Couch reprinted the same version in his edition of *The Oxford Book of Ballads*, with a few slight changes to punctuation and orthography in the interests of clarity – 'earthly' for 'ear'tly', 'bairn's' for 'bairnis', and so on.

When James Kinsley came along in 1969 to update *The*

---

10 He writes, 'I must not forget to add that it was sung to a tune sufficiently melancholy to express the surprise and sorrow of the deluded mother of the Phocine babe.' *Proceedings of the Society of Antiquaries of Scotland, Vol I*, 88, 1852, 86–88.

Oxford Book of Ballads, he criticised his predecessor Quiller-Couch for his occasional habit of piecing together lines from different variants to present the most poetically acceptable version, and for preferring 'lyrical' to 'narrative' ballads. Kinsley adds:

> Yet neither poetry nor even simplicity is as important as textual integrity. A true ballad 'text' is the recording of one auditory experience, one singer's song, and even the scrupulous translation of that on to the printed page is a kind of embalming. But if it must be done . . . there is . . . a moral as well as a technical difference between editing and fabrication.[11]

The difference between editing and fabrication is very important – but not actually relevant in the case of *The Great Silkie* which is indeed the recording of one auditory experience: Lieutenant Thomas's. With only a few tiny changes, Quiller-Couch faithfully transmitted this authentic version. So why did Kinsley ditch it? The real clue is when he quotes from an authority on ballads who published a book, *The Traditional Tunes of the Child Ballads*, in 1954: '"When is a ballad not a ballad?" asks Professor Bronson[12]. "When it has no tune."'[13]

Arthur Quiller-Couch could print no tune for *The Great Silkie of Sule Skerry* because although we know the old lady

11 *The Oxford Book of Ballads*, ed. James Kinsley, vi.
12 Bronson, Professor Bertrand Harris.
13 *The Oxford Book of Ballads*, ed. James Kinsley, vii.

of Snarra Voe sang the ballad, Lieutenant Thomas didn't or couldn't write the melody down. In James Kinsley's edition, however, *The Grey Selchie of Sule Skerry* comes with tune attached:

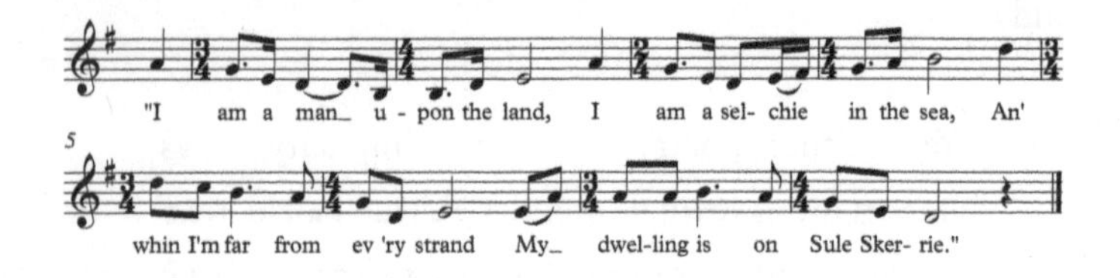

Where did he find it? I checked the notes and read: 'Air collected by Professor Otto Andersson in Orkney in 1938 and published, with text, in Budklaven,[14] xxvi (1947), 115; Mr Francis Collinson's arrangement is followed here.' So that was where *The Grey Selchie* came from. Impressed by Professor Bronson's clarion call, James Kinsley preferred an Orkney ballad of 1938 *with* a tune, over a Shetland ballad of 1852 without one. And that explained the modernised spellings: *The Grey Selchie* had been collected within the last thirty years.

But the plot thickens. Reading Kinsley's note again, I noticed that it does not claim Andersson collected the *words* of *The Grey Selchie* in 1938 – just the tune. Hunting further, I discovered that Andersson's contributor, John Sinclair of Flotta, Orkney, sang him *one stanza only*, the fifth[15] – the one I've called the core stanza. It is the one that begins, 'I am a man upon the land' and is similar in most versions. The

14 Budklaven is a Swedish journal.
15 Bronson, Bertrand Harris, *The Traditional Tunes of the Child Ballads*, 564.

full text of *The Grey Selchie* was contributed by the folklorist Anne Gilchrist,[16] who sent 'a full version of the words to Dr Andersson'[17] perhaps as late as 1947. Did she find it on Orkney? I can't discover. No evidence that I know of ties it directly to John Sinclair's tune. Yet if you're not very careful, it's easy to suppose the two were collected together. I see no reason why John Sinclair's Orkney tune should not have been earlier sung on Shetland. Still, an editor naturally wishes to take a different route from his predecessor. *The Grey Selchie* was a new(ish) discovery; it was at least associated with a tune, and compared with *The Great Silkie* it told a plainer and more coherent narrative – a thing Kinsley approved.

In *The Grey Selchie*, Hein Mailer the selkie father offers to wed the mother of his child (she refuses) and asks her to nurse his 'little wee son' for seven years, when he will return to claim him. In seven years he does return, and gives the mother a purse of gold. Again he offers to marry her and again she refuses,[18] and, in a development not seen in *The Great Silkie*, Hein Mailer puts a gold chain around his son's neck so that 'if ever he comes to the Norway lands' the mother will be able to recognise her son. Then, as in the Shetland version, he foretells the deaths of himself and his son at the hands of the gunner the woman will marry. This comes to pass:

---

16 Anne Gilchrist was a British folk song collector, 1863–1954.

17 Thomson, David, *The People of the Sea*, 212.

18 In Kinsley's version. In David Thomson's version, op. cit., the woman changes her mind and asks Hein Mailer to marry her and *he* refuses.

Oh she has gotten a gunner good,
And a gey good gunner it was he,
An' he gae'd out on a May morning,
An' he shot the son an' the grey selchie.[19]

Finally, the gunner brings back the golden chain to show his wife, who realises her son is dead and dies of a broken heart.

The Great Silkie (Shetland) and *The Grey Selchie* (Orkney) versions of the Sule Skerry ballad deal with the same story, the same set of circumstances, but the Shetland version is by far the more powerful. It's more concentrated, more compressed: this selkie has a harshness and otherness quite unlike that of 'good Hein Mailer'; he is 'a grumlie guest' who brings a waft of salt-sea terror as he appears; he has no name. By contrast, Hein Mailer is introduced as 'a good grey selchie': he addresses the woman with politeness, calling her 'pretty maid', and 'my dear', he offers to marry her; there's no sense that she's ever afraid of him, and the relational interplay between them nearly effaces their selkie child from the narrative. In *The Great Silkie* the beautiful verse in which the selkie and his little son delight in the summer-bright sea sharpens the tragedy of their deaths. There is no similar verse in *The Grey Selchie*, and the deaths of father and son at the end seem almost perfunctory, so that the ballad has to insist on the tragedy in a coda, four lines of conventional sorrow from the lady:

19 *The Oxford Book of Ballads*, ed. James Kinsley, 93: and also: Thomson, David, *The People of the Sea*, 213.

'Alas, alas this woeful fate
This weary fate that's been laid on me.'
And ance or twice she sobbed and sighed
An' her tender heart did brak in three.'[20]

Now the plot thickens even further. It turns out that there's another, much longer Orkney ballad – hardly even a ballad, more of an epic romance – called *The Play o' de Lathie Odivere* [The Play of the Lady Odivere] which, it has been claimed, is the *fons et origo*, the source from which all these variants sprang. It was put together and written down by the well-known Orkney folklorist and farmer W. Traill Dennison and published by him in 1893 in *The Scottish Antiquary, or, Northern Notes and Queries*. His introduction begins:

> In the olden times, Orcadians at their convivial meetings amused themselves by rude dramatical representations, in which lower animals often appeared on the scene. In these performances the menye-singers acted the principal part. They were professionals hired to sing, recite, or act for the entertainment of the company.
>
> This ballad was at one time represented as a drama by the menye-singers. This fact influenced me in adopting one of its old names, namely, play, in preference to other names by which the ballad was known – such as rhyme, ballan, teel.

---

20 *The Oxford Book of Ballads*, ed. James Kinsley, 93.

> The ballad was always divided into fits, but I have been told that its divisions were once known by another name, which I have been unable to discover.
>
> A few stanzas of the ballad appeared in the Transactions of the Scottish Antiquarian Society, communicated by Captain Thomas, R.N.,[21] and heard by him in Shetland.
>
> It is now well-nigh fifty years since I first heard parts of this ballad, for forty years I have been gathering up fragmentary scraps of it from many old people in different parts of Orkney.[22]

It sounds very interesting, exciting even, especially since Traill Dennison's 'fragmentary scraps' run, in their pieced-together form, for over ninety verses in five 'fits', or sections. They tell the story of a proud lady of Norway who rejects all her suitors until Odivere arrives. He has vowed by Odin ('him that hang on tree') that the lady will become his wife. (I supply a translation for readers who may find the Orkney dialect which Dennison uses obscure.)

He's coorted her, he's waded her
He's courted her, he's wedded her
An' dey wür blyth and blissfu' baith;
And they were happy and blissful both

21 Nice to know Lt. Thomson got his promotion.
22 Dennison, W. Traill, 'The Play o' de Lathie Odivere', *The Scottish Antiquary*, 53.

An' aye he bragged near an' far
And ever he bragged near and far
He wan his wife bae Odin's aith.[23]
He won his wife by Odin's oath.

Odivere then departs for 'Guthaland' (which Traill Dennison glosses as God's Land or the Holy Land') – 'The muckle pagan loons to slay'[24] and – returning – stops off at Muckle Garth (the Norse name for Constantinople, this means simply 'Great City' – the Big Apple, if you like!) where he beguiles himself with women, leaving his lady at home to mourn:

At Muckle Gerth he terried lang
At Muckle Garth he tarried long
Black sight on him for biddan dere
Bad luck on him for staying there
While sat i' dool her maids amang
While sat, in sorrow, among her maids,
Wi' tearfu' ee his lathie fair.
With tearful eye, his lady fair.[25]

This situation ends the first fit. At the beginning of the second, a strange knight arrives one evening at the Lady Odivere's castle door and demands shelter, claiming he brings news, and the gift of a gold ring, from Odivere.

---

23 Op. cit., 54.
24 'The muckle pagan loons': this less than polite phrase means something like 'the great big pagan fools'.
25 Ibid.

'A token fae dee husband dear
'A token from thy husband dear
I bring tae dee mae lathie fair,
I bring to thee, my lady fair
I left him weel, i' jolly cheer,
I left him well, in jolly cheer.
Dey ca' him noo, Sir Odivere.'
They call him now, Sir Odivere.'

Happy to hear this news, the lady feasts the knight ('Poor oot de best o' blude-reed wine!'). Soon, however, the knight insinuates (correctly) that Odivere has been unfaithful. Further, it turns out that the golden ring was once a token between the lady and this knight, who once were lovers.

'Ye ken, fair dame, tae me aye dear,
You know, fair dame, to me ever dear,
Lang syne ye gae dat ring tae me,
Long since you gave that ring to me,
An' on dis ring i' de mün licht clear
And on this ring in the moonlight clear,
Ye swüre forever mine tae be.'[26]
You swore forever mine to be.

The knight tells her he has never been able to forget her; the lady exclaims that it was Odin's oath which separated them, and in moments:

26 Dennison, W. Traill, 'The Play o' de Lathie Odivere', 55.

What happened neest ye need no' speer
What happened next you need not ask
In sooth I wus no dare to see.[27]
In truth I would not dare to see.

Let's stop here for a moment, less than half-way through, and take stock. There are things about this ballad that worry me, not least the intrusion of this rather coy narrative voice. Of course at first sight the entire poem looks archaic, but that is largely because W. Traill Dennison had a strong interest in the Orkney dialect – in which he wrote a number of excellent short stories – and he explains in his introduction that 'every word in the ballad added by me has been carefully chosen as the most suitable *and oldest* Orkney word I know' (my italics). He frankly admits that he's had to do a fair bit of darning and hole-filling: 'I have often had to fill in a word, sometimes a line, in order to make the sense clear or to complete the stanza.'

I suspect he's done a lot more than that. It seems clear to me that the ballad, at least *in this form*, is largely Traill Dennison's own construction. He himself tells us that all he had to work on were 'fragmentary scraps', and later speaks of his friend, Mrs Hiddleston, who 'never forgot the old tales and *scraps of verse* heard in the days of her childhood.' (Scraps again: my italics.)

There's a faux-medieval air that hangs about *The Play o' de Lathie Odivere* which just doesn't feel right for a traditional ballad, but feels exactly right for a mid-to-late nineteenth-

27 Ibid.

century romantic poem. There's too much padding: for example all of the italicised phrases here:

> '*Ye ken, fair dame, tae me aye dear,*
> Lang syne ye gae that ring tae me,
> *An' on this ring i' de mün licht clear*
> Ye swüre forever mine tae be.'

Traditional ballads are usually more laconic and less sentimental. 'Lang syne ye gae that ring tae me; Ye promised tae be true tae me' would be a closer match to the ballad formula. ('You swore forever to be mine' has 'Victorian reproach' stamped all over it.)

Not only that, but the simple plot of the Sule Skerry ballads is here elaborated almost beyond recognition. Traill Dennison would doubtless argue that the complex chicken should come before the simple egg – that a complicated 'play' degraded into a simple ballad. Such a process is certainly evident in the case of the fourteenth-century romance *Sir Orfeo*, which by some untraceable path gave rise to the far shorter and simpler ballad *King Orfeo,* collected in Shetland and published by Child in 1880. But why should the memorable Lady Odivere become an anonymous woman? Why are there so many narrative inconsistencies? We discover that Lady Odivere and the strange knight have kept tryst in the moonlight and exchanged rings, yet the 'play's' first few verses insist on the lady's virgin pride as she shows all of her suitors the door. It feels very much to me as if someone – not necessarily Traill Dennison – has taken the old ballad and decided to make more of a 'lover's triangle' of lady, selkie, and gunner-husband, focussing on sexual love and betrayal rather than on the parental love between mother, father and child. Instead of 'woman gets pregnant by selkie, bears his child, later remarries, husband shoots selkie and son', we have 'married lady plays her husband false by sleeping with former sweetheart and bearing his child – but her husband neglected her and was fooling about with other women, and she'd never have married him in the first place if he hadn't sworn the Odin oath'. This plot offers the advantage (to Victorian sensibilities) that the lady can wring her hands a lot and bewail her 'sinful shame'. The third fit, or section, is the overlay with the Sule Skerry ballad. I'll quote the first four stanzas:

I heard a lathie ba'an her bairn
I heard a lady lulling her child
An aye shü rockit; an' aye shü sang,
And aye she rocked it and aye she sang
An teuk sae hard upo de verse,
And took so hard upon the verse
Till de hert within her bothie rang.
Till the heart within her body rang

'Ba loo, ba loo, me bonnie bairn,
Ba loo, ba loo, my bonny child
Ba loo Lillie, ba loo lay,
Ba loo Lillie, ba loo lay
Sleep dü, me peerie bonnie budo!
Sleep thou, my little bonnie babe [?]

Du little kens dee mither's wae.

Little thou knows thy mother's woe.

'Aloor! I dinno ken dee faither

Alas! I do not know thy father

Aloor, aloor! Me waefu' sin!

Alas, alas! My woeful sin!

I dinno ken me bairn's faither

I do not know my child's father

Nor yet de land dat he lives in.

Nor yet the land that he lives in.

'Aloor! aloor! ca'd sall I be

Alas! Alas! I shall be called

A wicked woman bae a' men,

A wicked woman by all men

Dat I, a married wife, soud hae

That I, a married wife, should have

A bairn tae him I dünno ken.[28]

A child by one I do not know.

This has the appearance of a genuine, traditional ballad – with ornamental extras. 'Aloor, aloor!' the lady wails, worried about what the neighbours will think. Next:

Dan ap an' spak a grimly guest

Then up and spoke a grimly guest

28 Op. cit., 55.

Dat stud sae lech at her bed feet,
That stood so low [?] at her bed foot
'O here am I, dee bairn's faither,
'O here am I, thy child's father,
Alto I'm no' dee husband sweet.'[29]
Although I'm not thy husband sweet.'

Over the next two verses they have a conversation about Odivere – 'a guid, guid man' – and the 'grimly guest' offers to return in six months' time to pay his child's nursing fee. The lady asks his name (though having exchanged rings with him in the moonlight and subsequently slept with him, you'd think she might have asked before):

'Noo, for de luve I bür tae dee,
Now, for the love I bore to thee,
A luve dats brought me muckle sheem,
A love that's brought me great shame,
O tell me whar dee heem may be,
O tell me where your home may be,
An tell me true dee vera neem?'[30]
And tell me true your own true name?

('A love that's brought me great shame' – again the poet, whoever he was, is harping on public and social rather than private and emotional consequences.) The selkie tells her his

29 Ibid.
30 Op. cit., 55.

name is San Imravoe and that he is a selkie earl of high degree, with a thousand or more selkies at his command to whom his word is law. And yes, he comes from Sule Skerry:

'San Imravoe hit is me neem,
San Imravoe it is my name,
I gong on land; an' sweem on see,
I walk on land, and swim on sea,
Amang de ranks o' selkie folk
Among the ranks of selkie folk
I am a yarl o' hich degree.
I am an earl of high degree.

I am a man upo' de land,
I am a man upon the land,
I am a selkie i' de sea;
I am a selkie in the sea;
Me heem it is de Soola-Skerry,
My home it is the Sule Skerry
An' a' dat's dere is under me.
And all that's there is under me.

Mair or a thoosan selkie folk,
More than a thousand selkie folk
Tae me a willin service gae;
To me a willing service pay
An' I am king o' a' de folk,
And I am king of all the folk

An' la' tae dem is what I say.[31]

And law to them is what I say.

Briefly to tell you what happens in the rest of the ballad: when the selkie claims his son, the lady ties a golden chain around the seal-child's neck, a chain which we are only now told had been a wedding gift from Odivere. (In *The Grey Selchie* it is Hein Mailer the selkie father who gives the chain to his son: there is no chain at all in *The Great Silkie.*) In the fourth fit Odivere comes home and feasts till, worried he and his men will grow 'fat as butterballs' he suggests some exercise hunting otters on the shore. During the hunt Odivere kills a seal wearing the gold chain, which he recognises as the one he gave his wife. He confronts her; she laments aloud the death of her son; Odivere calls her a slut, and they quarrel. In a lively stanza the lady grabs the chain and slashes Odivere over the head with it, crying 'go tak ye that, ye ill-tongued tike', and he locks her up in a tower.

In the fifth 'fit', the 'Ting' or Orkney assembly sentences Lady Odivere to death by burning, but the day before this is due, her selkie lover San Imravoe comes to the rescue. He and his selkies call all the whales in the North Sea to gather in the bay and seeing them (it's an Orkney ballad, remember) Odivere and his men rush to the shore, raising the stirring shout, 'Whals, whals! i' ilka bey an' voe!' ('Whales, whales! in every bay and inlet!') They don't manage to kill a single whale, however, and on their return the Lady Odivere

---

31 Ibid.

has gone, no doubt to join her lover in the sea. The ballad concludes,

An Oddiver's a lanely man,
And Odivere's a lonely man
An weary o' his sicker skathe,
And weary of his deadly hurt
An aye an' sare he rues the day
And aye and sore he rues the day
He ever tük de Odin aith.
He ever took the Odin oath.

Tae menye-singers tanks we gae,
To menye-singers thanks we give,
Tae menye-singers drink we a';
To menye-singers drink we all;
Wür foys dey wür no wirt a strae
Our feasts would not be worth a straw
Withoot der sangs an' ballans bra.[32]
Without their songs and ballads fine.

I have to confess I was really reluctant, on first reading *The Play o' de Lathie Odivere*, to accept it as what W. Traill Dennison claims it to be, the origin of *The Great Silkie of Sule Skerry*. In its way it's magnificent, but it troubled me. I wasn't convinced. I questioned myself. Why shouldn't he be right? After all, there are some very long ballads, though maybe none as long as

32 Op. cit., 57.

this – and anyway, as Traill Dennison justly points out, this isn't a ballad so much as an entertainment – a play – which would have been part-acted, part sung by what Traill Dennison calls the menye-singers.[33] Therein lies a clue. If the Orkney menye-plays were anything like the mumming plays of England, all the parts would have been acted and sung by men, and would have included a great deal of burlesque which could account for the slapstick verse in which Odivere's lady turns on him:

> She's whiped de chain fae de selkie's hars
> She's snatched the chain from the selkie's neck
> An' waped hid on Odie's croon,
> And whacked it down on Odie's crown
> Gae tak ye that, ye ill-tongued tike,
> 'Go take you that, you ill-tongued dog,
> An' keep hid for a pertin boon.
> And keep it [*ie: the blow*] for a parting gift.'

The menye-play or mumming play theory may also account for the presence of some un-ballad-like references to Sir Odivere fighting pagan knights in the Holy Land. There is often a 'Turkish Champion' in the Saint George mumming plays, and one can easily imagine an interlude in *The Play o' the Lathie Odivere* in which some of the menye-players may have put on a sword fight or sword dance to entertain the audience while the singers rested.

33 Like the *minnesingers* of medieval Germany. In a fabulous story, 'The Ballad Singer' George Mackay Brown imagines 'The Lady Odivere' being sung in an Orkney hall some time in the sixteenth century. It can be found in *An Orkney Tapestry*, 1969.

A successful mumming play requires action (and plenty of it), colourful characters and simple, strong relationships. It needs to be obvious, not subtle. Fighting, betrayal, jealousy, revenge and a splash of comedy will do very well. Many of the jigsaw fragments of verse which Traill Dennison and his collaborator Mrs Hiddleton puzzled over must, as he suggests, have come from a menye-play. That doesn't mean – in fact it's unlikely to mean – that the menye-play was the origin of the Sule Skerry ballads. To me it seems more probable that someone took an existing menye-play (about a crusading knight, his lady and her lover), borrowed the selkie ballad and cobbled it into the plot, generating a number of inconsistencies and absurdities. The strange knight in the first 'fit', for example, who brings the lady news of Odivere's activities overseas, would make far better narrative sense as one of Odivere's companions arriving home ahead of him, than he does as a seal. And if we are to believe that the golden chain was a gift from Odivere to his lady, and therefore important evidence of her later betrayal, why aren't we shown him giving it to her before he departs on crusade? Traditional ballads don't usually overlook such details.

Whether or not this is what happened, it's certain that Traill Dennison used the fragmentary material he found to create what is effectively a romantic poem in the grand tradition of Sir Walter Scott.[34] As such, it works very well on the whole, apart from those lines into which he has injected a Victorian morality

---

34 'Traill Dennison is the source for most of the Orcadian material [on selkies] and it's clear that he romanticised and systematised his material to quite a degree': Dr. Andrew Jennings, *The Finnfolk*, Address to the Shetland Museum, 25 March 2010, accessed 15.12.15: www.uhi.ac.uk/en/research-enterprise/cultural/centre-for-nordic-studies/conferences/the-finnfolk.

which sits uneasily with the ballad and mumming-play elements. Especially in the third 'fit' or section, where the lady rocks her child, he consistently directs the attention of listener or reader to the guilty 'sin' of the married woman who has had a child out of wedlock. In *The Great Silkie* and *The Grey Selchie* there is no hint of guilt, only sorrow on the part of a single mother for her fatherless bairn. A reason for supposing that Traill Dennison was himself personally responsible for these interpolations is that one more version of the Sule Skerry ballad exists. Its source is 'the minister of North Ronaldsay, Orkney', who in 1859 sent it to the folklorist John Campbell of Islay,[35] among whose manuscripts it lay unpublished until David Thomson reproduced it in *The People of the Sea*. It is therefore the second oldest version we know of, after the Shetland version published by Lt. Thomas in 1852. It was collected on Orkney, and it corresponds closely to parts of Traill Dennison's version of 1893, including the name of the selkie himself – but with a more modern vocabulary and with none of the intruding, morally judgemental lines. Entitled simply *Sealchie Song*, it begins:

I heard a Mither baing her bairn,
An' aye she rockit an she sang,
She took sae hard upon the verse
Till the heart within her body rang.

'Oh row cradle and go cradle,
An ay sleep thon my bairn within

35 John Francis Campbell, 1821–1885.

O little ken I my bairn's faither,
Or yet the land that he liggs in.

O up then spake a grimly Ghost
A aye sae laigh at her bed's feet,
'O here am I thy bairns faither
Although I'm nae thy luve sae sweet,

Jo[36] Immrannoe it is my name,
Jo Immrannoe they do ca' me,
An' my lands they lie baith braid an' wide,
Amang the rocks o' Sule Skerry.

There is no golden chain in *Sealchie Song*, however, and it shares with all the other ballad versions the woman's gunner-husband whose shot kills, in this version, the woman herself. The ballad ends on a warning:

Jo Immrannoe an' his young son
Wi heavy hearts took tae the sea
Let a' that live on mortal Lird
Ne'er mell[37] wi Selchies o' the sea.[38]

What does all this demonstrate? Once again, that there's no

---

36 'Jo': Scots word for 'sweetheart' (as in Burns' poem 'John Anderson, my jo, John').
37 Meddle.
38 Thomson, David, *The People of the Sea*, 215. The word 'Lird' is unknown to me.

such thing as an 'original' ballad, folk or fairy tale, and that we need to look closely at who is telling us the story and why. Traill Dennisson, to whom we undoubtedly owe the preservation of many interesting tales, legends and fragments of verse, was primarily interested in recording and promoting the Orcadian dialect. As James Kinsley remarked, with Quiller-Couch in his sights, there is a fine line to tread between editing and fabrication (though fabrication is an unkind term). Like many a nineteenth-century collector Traill Dennison wanted to present not fragments and scraps but a finished piece of work. In order to do so he had to fabricate, he had to weave together his material, and *The Play o' de Lathie Odivere* becomes a sort of flag he waves for Orcadian culture, history and literature. It's greatly enjoyable, but should be regarded as an interpretive, creative reconstruction, like the restoration of Carcassonne by Viollet-le-Duc:[39] a Victorian take on the Middle Ages.

The Great Silkie of Sule Skerry, 1852. *Sealchie Song*, 1859. *The Play o' de Laithie Odivere*, 1893. *The Grey Selchie of Sule Skerry*, 1938–47 . . . Summed up, what stays with me from all of these? It is their expression of the vigour and wildness of the northern seas, it's this:

> I am a man upo' the lan'
> An' I am a Silkie in the sea;
> And when I'm far and far frae lan'
> My dwelling is in Sule Skerrie.

---

39 In his restoration of the walled city of Carcassonne, Viollet-le-Duc added conical roofs to the towers, typical of northern rather than southern French medieval architecture.

Jorinda and Joringel: Owls and Flowers

There's a story in *The Mabinogion* about a girl who is changed into an owl. The magicians Gwydion and Math ap Mathonwy create her out of flowers for Lleu Llaw Gyffes whose mother has cursed him never to have a human wife. They take 'the flowers of the oak, and the flowers of the broom, and the flowers of the meadowsweet, and from those they conjured the fairest and most beautiful maiden that anyone had ever seen. And they baptised her in the way that they did at that time, and named her Blodeuedd.'[1]

Deed done, curse circumvented. Blodeuedd is presented to Lleu. Nobody has asked her what *she* wants, however, and one day when Lleu is away she meets the handsome young man Gronw Pebr. The two fall in love and plot to murder Lleu so that they can be together. At the moment of his death, Lleu is transformed into an eagle. Math restores him to his human shape, and Gwydion pursues Blodeuedd and transforms her into an owl.

---

1 *The Mabinogion*, tr. Sioned Davies, 58.

> '[Y]ou will never dare show your face in daylight for fear of all the birds. And all the birds will be hostile towards you . . . You shall not lose your name, however, but shall always be called Blodeuwedd.'[2] *Blodeuwedd* is 'owl' in today's language. And for that reason the birds hate the owl: and the owl is still called *Blodeuwedd*.[3]

Commenting on the tale, Sioned Davies explains that the name 'changes from Blodeuedd ('flowers') to Blodeuwedd ('flower-face') to reflect the image of the bird.'[4] The white face of the barn owl does, in fact, look rather like two huge white daisies crushed together.

Blodeuedd is a girl made from flowers and turned into an owl. In the Grimms' fairy tale *Jorinda and Joringel*[5] a girl is turned into a bird by an owl-woman – and released by the touch of a flower. Here's what happens.

In the middle of a dark forest is an ancient castle inhabited by an old woman who turns into a cat or night-owl by day, assuming her own form only when evening comes. She lures wild birds and beasts to her, and kills and eats them.

> If anyone came within one hundred paces of the castle he was obliged to stand still and could not

---

2 Op. cit., 63.

3 *Blodeuwedd* does not appear to be a word for 'owl' in modern Welsh, however.

4 Op. cit., 244.

5 'Jorinda and Joringel', KHM 69, *Grimm's Fairy Tales*, 339.

> stir from the spot until she bade him be free. But whenever an innocent maiden came within this circle, she changed her into a bird and shut her up in a wickerwork cage, and carried the cage into a room in the castle. She had about seven thousand cages of rare birds in the castle.[6]

A betrothed young couple, Jorinda and Joringel, walk into the forest in order to be alone together. Though Joringel warns his sweetheart that they must take care not to stray close to the castle, everything should be wonderful in this glowing sunset wood: 'It was a beautiful evening. The sun shone brightly between the trunks of the trees into the dark green of the forest, and the turtledoves sang mournfully upon the beech trees.' But for some reason the young lovers are sorrowful – 'as sad as though they were about to die'. In this strange mood,

> [T]hey looked around them, and were quite at a loss, for they did not know which way they should go home. The sun was still half above the mountain and half under. Joringel looked through the bushes, and saw the old walls of the castle close at hand.
>
> He was horror-stricken and filled with deadly fear. Jorinda was singing: 'My little bird with the necklace red Sings sorrow, sorrow, sorrow.

6 Ibid.

> He sings that the little dove must soon be dead.
> Sings sorrow, sor— jug, jug, jug.'[7]

The sun has set, Jorinda has been changed into a nightingale, and 'a screech owl with glowing eyes flew three times round about her, and three times cried "to-whoo, to-whoo, to-whoo!"' Unable to speak or move, Joringel sees the owl fly into a thicket and emerge as a crooked old woman 'with large red eyes' who catches the nightingale and takes it away.

Later that evening the enchantress returns later and releases Joringel with the cryptic words, 'Greet you, Zachiel. If the moon shines on the cage, Zachiel, let him loose at once,' but she refuses to release Jorinda and tells Joringel he will never see his sweetheart again. Joringel goes sadly away. Working as a shepherd in a nearby village, he dreams of a blood-red flower containing a dew-drop as big as a pearl, with which he can open the doors of the castle and the cage. After a nine-day search he finds the flower, and sets Jorinda and all the other maidens free.

The Grimm brothers took the tale almost verbatim from the deeply Romantic semi-fictional autobiography of Johann Heinrich Jung, *The Life of Heinrich Stilling*, published in 1777. Writing throughout in the third person, Jung tells how one day, in the forest gathering firewood, the eleven-year-old Heinrich asks his Aunt Marie for a story. '"Tell me, aunt, once more," said Heinrich, "the tale of Joringel and Jorinde."' His aunt is happy to oblige, and when she has finished, Heinrich sits 'as if

7 Op. cit., 339–40.

petrified – his eyes fixed and his mouth half-open. "Aunt!" said he, at length, "it is enough to make one afraid in the night!" "Yes," said she, "I do not tell these tales at night, otherwise I should be afraid myself.'"[8]

It's rather lovely to have this account of the story actually being told and to see its effect on child and storyteller. It is placed in this context, however, because of what happens next. Having gone deeper into the woods, Heinrich's grandfather comes back to tell them how he saw a bright light between the trees, 'just as when the sun rises in the morning'. Led by the light, he sees a vision of the brilliant castles and gardens of heaven, and meets his daughter Dora, Heinrich's dead mother, who tells him he will soon join her in 'our eternal habitation'. The dark forest, failing sunset, ancient castle and evil enchantress of the fairy tale are thus deliberately contrasted with the brilliant sunrise, shining castles and angelic beings of heaven.

This then, like *The Juniper Tree*, is a literary version of a traditional tale, and since the rest of the 'autobiography' is full of poetical and mystical references to doves, nightingales, morning and evening sun, rings, dewdrops and death, I would guess that the moody music of the opening few paragraphs – sorrowful lovers, setting sun and mourning doves – is Johann Heinrich Jung's own. Does this make the story less authentic? I don't see it that way. Tellers of traditional tales have always enriched, altered and embellished them as they see fit, and a story written down will always be different from the same tale told aloud.

---

8 *The Autobiography of Heinrich Stilling*, tr. S Jackson, 22.

What does the story mean? Why are the lovers so sad? Is it because they know they'll grow old and die, because evening is here and the day nearly over, because their young love may not last and the sun is already half beneath the mountain? Are they afraid of mortality, the grave, symbolised by the grim stone walls of the castle whose shadow immobilises them, and the old owl-woman whose voice is a lament?

Or is the owl-woman associated with Athena of classical mythology, goddess of wisdom, whose emblem was the owl? Discussing the tale with me, the author Susan Price thought this might be so, writing:

> My impression is a little different. For one, the old woman is associated with the owl, which associates her with Athena. She's also a huntress, who seems to prize and cage (or guard) unmarried girls, which associates her with Artemis. Both these goddesses had their darker, Death sides.
>
> The youngsters are lost in a wood – *wode*[9] within this wood. The forest has long been associated with the dangers and traps of life, some of them sexual – but mostly, I think, to do with 'losing one's way' or losing one's self. There's also a tradition of the girl about to be married mourning her single life: her happy life at home with her parents. She's about to launch into

9 'Wode within this wood': *Midsummer Night's Dream*, Act 2 Sc 1. Wode: adj: 'mad', OE. *wōd.*

> adult life, with all its responsibility and cares. The owl-woman snatches her away from all this and fastens her securely in a cage – but doesn't otherwise mistreat her. The old woman also frees the young man without harming him and tells him that if he does the right thing, he can free the girl. I think the old woman is a kind of marriage counsellor![10]

This is a thought-provoking comment and a good illustration of the ways in which fairy tales can be differently interpreted.

Flowers and owls . . . owls and flowers . . . a blood-red flower with a pearl-sized drop of dew at its heart.[11] To modern eyes the sexual imagery is clear, yet there is also a folkloric explanation. In his *Teutonic Mythology*, Jacob Grimm describes a flower known as the 'wonderflower' which can be used to gain entrance to hidden treasure.

> To get into the mountain in which it is usually concealed, one usually needs a plant or root to clear the way, to burst the door.
>
> The folktales simply call it a beautiful *wonderflower*, which the favoured person finds and sticks in his hat: all at once entrance and exit stand open for him to the treasure of the mountain. If inside the cavern he has filled his pockets,

10 Susan Price, personal communication.

11 In *The Autobiography of Heinrich Stilling* the flower holds not a dew-drop but a real pearl.

> and bewildered at the sight of the valuables, has laid aside his hat, a warning voice rings in his ear as he departs: '*Forget not the best!*' But it is too late. *The iron door shuts with a bang, hard upon his heel*, in a twinkling all has disappeared, and the road is never to be found again.
>
> The flower is commonly said to be blue, the colour most proper to gods and spirits, yet also I find '*purple* flower' and '*white* flower' mentioned. Sometimes it is called *schlüsselblume* (key-flower), because it locks the vault, and as a symbol of the key-wearing white woman, whom the bunch of keys befits as old mistress and housekeeper, and who has likewise power to unlock the treasure.[12]

This imagery of flowers and keys is obviously also open to a Freudian interpretation. If Joringel's flower is a key-flower, to use it he needs to circumvent or appease the guardian of the treasure. Perhaps, in this interpretation, the old woman is an aspect of Jorinda herself.

Then what is the owl doing in this tale? What does it symbolise – wisdom or death? It seems likely that the 'wise owl' entered northern European folklore rather late, via classical education, and was originally known as a bird of death. In *The Mabinogion* the owl is a hated outcast, a bird of ill omen rather than of wisdom, and this is supported by Chaucer, 'The

12 Grimm, Jacob, *Teutonic Mythology*, Vol. III, 971–2 (the italics are Grimm's).

oule ek, that of deth the bode bringeth'; Shakespeare, 'Whilst the scritch-owle, scritching loud, Puts the wretch that lies in woe, In remembrance of a shrowd'; Gilbert White, 'From this screaming probably arose the common people's imaginary species of screech-owl, which they superstitiously think attends the windows of dying persons'; and even John Ruskin, 'Whatever wise people may say of them, I at least have found the owl's cry always prophetic of mischief to me.'[13] Moreover, in a variant of the tale noted by the brothers Grimm, it is a crow the old woman turns into – another bird associated with death.

In Alan Garner's 1967 novel *The Owl Service*, which is based on the story of Blodeuedd, the destructive force of the ancient legend is stored in a set of patterned dinner plates hidden in the attic of an old Welsh house. The stylised pattern can be perceived in two different ways, as either owls or flowers, and the plates act as a kind of battery, discharging power through the teenage Alison, who channels Blodeuedd. 'I said to Roger that I thought the plates were batteries and you were the wires,' says the Welsh boy, Gwyn. 'She wants to be flowers, but you make her owls,' says another character, Huw. The alternating owl/flower binary means not only that the emotional pattern of the legend keeps repeating down the centuries, but that the teenage characters switch between positive and negative constructions of themselves.

In *Jorinda and Joringel*, the constrictive power of age is represented by an owl and the liberating power of youth by a

---

13 Opie, Iona and Tatem, Moira, *A Dictionary of Superstitions*, 295.

flower. Years ago in my early twenties I was walking through London with a friend. We were laughing and chatting, and a middle-aged woman passing by leaned over and said to us in a low voice but with extraordinary venom, 'One day you'll be like me.' As a *memento mori* it was quite something and we both shivered, but we agreed later that we never would be like her. We would never, ever be that bitter.

That brush with mortality has stayed with me, however, and I have to recognise at least the existence of those dark emotions – envy of youth, anger at old age, fear of death. 'When [the old woman] saw Joringel coming she was angry, very angry, and scolded, and spat poison and gall at him, but she could not come within two paces of him.'[14] In the end the old woman is powerless against the sexual potency of youth. Fairy tales are emotional amplifiers. We look into them as if into old, dimly-silvered mirrors, and see ourselves and the world around us oddly changed. Analysing a fairy tale can be a deeply interesting intellectual exercise, but that is not what the tale itself is for. It works as music does, directly on our feelings. *Jorinda and Joringel* is short and there's hardly any plot, but it is intense. It takes the dark emotions and transmutes them, leaving us to remember the beauty of the forest, the sadness of the lovers and the strange little song Jorinda sings.

Like age, looking wistfully back on a time of flowers.

14 'Jorinda and Joringel', KHM 69, *Grimm's Fairy Tales*, 341.

Bluebeard, Mr Fox and the Bloody Chamber

I've never liked the story of *Bluebeard*.[1] I don't know anyone who does. It's a nasty, charmless piece of blood and thunder. As a fairy tale, its content is exceedingly adult. Its effect depends almost totally on how much the reader or listener can enjoy the voyeuristic suspense of wondering if and when Bluebeard's wife will die.

The relationship is abusive from the start. Bluebeard has already had several wives, all of whom have all mysteriously disappeared. The young woman knows this, but since he has 'several fine houses both in town and country, a good deal of silver and gold plate, embroider'd furniture, and coaches gilt all over with gold', people still receive him and visit him, and she marries him anyway. Once she is his wife, Bluebeard gives her the keys to his country house, explaining that they open the best rooms and strong boxes. Then he points out one in particular:

---

1 'La Barbe Bleu', one of Charles Perrault's *Histoires ou Contes du Temps Passé*, 1697.

> . . . this little one here, it is the key of the closet at the end of the great gallery on the ground floor. Open them all, go into all and every one except this little closet, which I forbid you, and forbid you in such a manner, that if you happen to open it, there is nothing but what you may expect from my just anger and resentment.[2]

He's setting her up, of course. Anyway this sort of threat should always raise eyebrows: disobedience of an apparently random prohibition cannot provoke 'just' anger. He means to kill her, but he wants to justify it to himself, put her in the wrong, make it her fault. It's as though Bluebeard sees himself as God, forbidding the Apple of the Tree of Knowledge to Eve.

Like Eve, Bluebeard's wife disobeys: she can't resist the temptation to see what's inside the 'closet' – not a cupboard, as we would now think it, but a small, private chamber. Once her husband has taken himself off, supposedly on business but actually of course to test her, her curiosity is such that, leaving her guests 'without considering that it was very uncivil of her to leave her company',

> . . . she went down a back pair of stairs, and with such an excessive haste, that she had like to have broken her neck . . .

Lowering herself to use *the back stairs*, which are for *servants*?

2 Opie, Iona and Peter, 'Bluebeard', *The Classic Fairy Tales*, 138 et seq.

Dear me! One senses Perrault, to whom we owe the tale, tutting. He disapproves of her. In fact his attitude to her is uncomfortably similar to Bluebeard's own: he's half of Bluebeard's mind. She may not deserve to be murdered, but she's partly to blame, isn't she? She married Bluebeard when she should have known better. She was told not to open the door, but she disobeyed. If she'd behaved with propriety, if she'd done what she was told, if she'd stayed with her guests . . . er . . . she might still be married to a mass murderer?

Outside the door she dithers, 'thinking upon her husband's orders, and considering what unhappiness might attend her were she disobedient; but the temptation was so strong she could not overcome it.' Unlocking the door, she discovers the bloodied corpses of Bluebeard's previous disobedient wives, gets blood on the key and – instead of running away – awaits Bluebeard's return in passive terror, even welcoming him and doing 'all she could to convince him she was extremely glad of his speedy return'.

A distasteful episode follows. Bluebeard examines the key and with the twisted mind-set of the true misogynistic serial killer blames his wife for what he's going to do to her:

> The *Blue Beard*, having very attentively consider'd it, said to his Wife, how comes this blood upon the key? I don't know, said the poor Woman paler than death. You don't know, replied the *Blue Beard*, I know very well, you were resolved to go into the closet, were you not? Very well, Madam,

> you shall go in, and take your place among the ladies you saw there.

Throwing herself at his feet, the woman begs for life 'with all the signs of a true repentance, and that she would never more be disobedient. She would have melted a rock, so beautiful and sorrowful was she, but the *Blue Beard* had a heart harder than the hardest rock!' (In this image of the woman – prostrate, terrified, submissive, pleading – Perrault indulges his readers in a little pornographic thrill.) Bluebeard grants her a quarter of an hour in which to say her prayers, and rather improbably leaves her alone. She asks her sister to climb the tower and look for the arrival of her brothers, who had promised to arrive that day. '*Anne, Sister Anne,*' she calls, '*dost thou see nothing coming?*' Three times her sister answers her: '*I see nothing but the sun that makes a dust and the grass that grows green*', but at the last possible moment her brothers arrive in time to prevent her murder. They run their swords through Bluebeard's body and leave him dead.

As traditional as they come, yes? Passive, stupid heroine, endangered by her own curiosity, rescued by males?

I don't know about you, but I feel as if I need a break from all this, so I'll tell you about anti-fairy tales. An anti-fairy tale is a critical term for a tale which 'takes aspects of the fairy-tale genre and re-imagines, subverts, inverts, deconstructs or satirises elements of them to present an alternate narrative interpretation, outcome of morality.'[3] An example might be

---

3 From 'Anti-Tales: The Uses of Disenchantment Symposium',

Roald Dahl's version of Little Red Riding Hood, in which Red Riding Hood whips a pistol from her knickers and shoots the wolf dead. It's a useful critical concept, but defining the anti-fairy tale is as tricky as everything else to do with the genre: like trying to catch your own shadow. (You won't succeed. Or if by some nursery fireside magic you do, don't try and stick it to yourself with anything as slippery as soap; get a little girl to sew it to you with teeny tiny stitches and a sharp steel needle.) It depends what you think the traditional fairy tale includes. And excludes. After all, *Bluebeard* itself could be viewed as the anti-tale to *Beauty and the Beast.* In one, a woman marries a rich man who turns out to be a murderer. In the other, a woman goes to live with a threatening Beast who turns out to be gentle and kind. It's best to look at the whole thing out of the corner of your eye while pretending to be absorbed in something else.

Angela Carter's short story 'The Bloody Chamber'[4] is the modern, adult, complex anti-fairy tale version of *Bluebeard.* A young woman marries a rich Marquis she does not love, who turns out to be keen on sadistic pornography. When she too investigates the room she's been told to avoid, the male hero (the blind piano-tuner who loves her) is unable to save her, and in a final twist her mother arrives and shoots the Marquis dead. Though the heroine is still infantilised, at least the mature woman triumphs. Female power at last!

Yes: but now let's look at the English fairy tale *Mr Fox*, which

---

posted June 30 2010 on the Sussex Folkore Centre website. I am indebted to Dr John P. Pazdziora and Defne Çizakca for introducing me to the concept of anti-tales.

4 Carter, Angela, *The Bloody Chamber and Other Stories.*

is old enough to have been familiar to Shakespeare's audience: Benedick quotes from it in *Much Ado About Nothing*.[5] This is how it begins.

> Lady Mary was young, and Lady Mary was fair. She had two brothers, and more lovers than she could count. But of all of them, the bravest and most gallant, was a Mr Fox, whom she met when she was down at her father's country-house. No one knew who he was; but he was certainly brave, and surely rich, and of all her lovers, Lady Mary cared for him alone. At last it was agreed between them that they should be married. Lady Mary asked Mr Fox where they should live, and he described to her his castle, and where it was; but, strange to say, did not ask her or her brothers to come and see it.
>
> So one day, near the wedding day, when her brothers were out and Mr Fox was away for a day or two on business, as he said, Lady Mary set out for Mr Fox's castle.[6]

Lady Mary's female curiosity takes her into the woods looking for the castle which her betrothed suitor is so inexplicably reluctant to show her. Perhaps she's already a little suspicious?

She finds the castle deserted: 'a fine strong house . . . with

---

5 'Like the old tale, my Lord, "It is not so and it was not so, but indeed, God forbid it should be so"': *Much Ado About Nothing*, I,i.

6 Jacobs, Joseph, 'Mr Fox,' *English Fairy Tales*, 148 et seq.

high walls and a deep moat.' Over the gateway, words are carved in the stone: '**Be bold, be bold**.' It could be any knight's motto, but the words change as she proceeds. Over the castle doorway is written, '**Be bold, be bold, but not too bold**.' Still she goes on, through a hall and up a staircase:

> Still she went on, till she came into the halls, and
> went up the broad stairs till she came to a door in
> the gallery, over which was written:
> **Be bold, be bold, but not too bold**
> **Lest that your heart's blood should run cold.**
> But Lady Mary was a brave one, she was, and she
> opened the door . . .

'Lady Mary was a brave one'. How different this story is from its analogue, *Bluebeard*! Throughout the tale, Lady Mary has agency. She becomes engaged to Mr Fox because she cares for him. She asks him pertinent, reasonable questions. When he doesn't respond in a satisfactory way, she goes to find out for herself (and by herself). Instead of hysterical excitement and a helter-skelter descent of the back stairs, Lady Mary calmly and systematically explores Mr Fox's castle and ascends the broad main staircase. She's in control. And – she's brave.

> . . . she opened the door, and what do you think
> she saw? Why, bodies and skeletons of beautiful
> young ladies all stained with blood.

Does she scream and swoon and sink to the floor? No. She 'thought it was high to get out of that horrid place, and she closed the door, went through the gallery, and was just going down the stairs' when, on the point of escape, she sees Mr Fox returning to the castle at the head of a band of robbers, dragging an unconscious woman behind him. Hiding behind a barrel, she witnesses Mr Fox tugging at a diamond ring which sparkles on the hand of the 'poor young lady'. It won't come, so he draws his sword and chops the lady's hand off. It springs into the air and falls where Lady Mary is hiding. Mr Fox searches but cannot find it, so he goes on up the stairs to the Bloody Chamber.

> As soon as she heard him pass through the gallery, Lady Mary crept out of the door, down through the gateway, and ran home as fast as she could.

Lady Mary gets away safe. She has rescued herself, without any need of male assistance. But we're only half-way through: there's more.

> It happened that the very next day the marriage contract of Lady Mary and Mr Fox was to be signed, and there was a splendid breakfast before that. And when Mr Fox was seated at table opposite Lady Mary, he looked at her. 'How pale you are this morning, my dear.' 'Yes' said she, 'I had a bad night's rest last night. I had horrible dreams.' 'Dreams go by contraries,' said Mr Fox;

> 'but tell us your dreams, and your sweet voice will make the time pass till the happy hour comes.'
>
> 'I dreamed,' said Lady Mary, 'that I went yestermorn to your castle . . .'

And she begins to tell Mr Fox the very story we've already heard. The tables have turned, and now Mr Fox is at a disadvantage. *We* know that *Lady Mary* knows just what sort of villain Mr Fox truly is – but *he* doesn't. The mounting tension of the first half of the story was created by the increasingly disturbing mottoes. As Lady Mary recounts her 'dream' and repeats these mottoes, Mr Fox responds with increasingly vehement denials.

> '. . . I found it in the woods, with high walls, and a deep moat, and over the gateway was written:
>
> **Be bold, be bold.'**
>
> 'But it is not so, nor it was not so,' said Mr Fox.

He repeats this mantra for each of the mottoes, but when Lady Mary reaches the discovery of the Bloody Chamber, he adds moral intensity to his denial:

> 'It is not so, nor it was not so. And God forbid it should be so,' said Mr Fox.
>
> 'I then dreamed that I rushed down the gallery, and just as I was going down the stairs, I saw you, Mr Fox, coming up to the hall door,

> dragging after you a poor young lady, rich and beautiful.'
>
> 'It is not so, nor it was not so. And God forbid it should be so,' said Mr Fox.

You can feel him wriggling. He doesn't know what to think. Can his fiancée's account really be just a dream? It must be – she can't know anything! Surely she wouldn't behave like this if she did? She hasn't actually accused him. This is their wedding breakfast! She'll be married to him in an hour. He has a chance! He's got to convince her this is all nonsense. And anyway, who would believe her?

> 'And, as you passed me, Mr Fox, I thought I saw you try and get off her diamond ring, and when you could not, Mr Fox, it seemed to me in my dream, that you out with your sword and hacked off the poor lady's hand to get the ring.'
>
> 'It is not so, and it was not so, and God forbid it should be so,' said Mr Fox, and was going to say something else as he rose from his seat –

For this is unbearable; he needs to put an end to this piece of female folly; he needs to interrupt the inexorable repetition of his name, 'Mr, Fox, Mr Fox, Mr Fox', in connection with these terrible deeds. But before he can speak, Lady Mary lets all her carefully controlled anger flash out. She cries,

> 'But it is so, and it was so. Here's hand and ring

> I have to show,' and pulled out the lady's hand from her dress and pointed it straight at Mr Fox.
>
> At once, her brothers and their friends drew their swords and cut Mr Fox into a thousand pieces.

She took the severed hand home with her! We weren't told – we didn't know! This is the final surprise. Lady Mary has kept the proof, the incontrovertible proof that her so-called dream is true, and uses the hand of the murdered girl to accuse the murderer. She has orchestrated the entire revenge and no one can doubt that when her brothers rise 'and cut Mr Fox into a thousand pieces' they are not Lady Mary's rescuers, but her agents.

I would never tell *Bluebeard* to children. I think it is completely unsuitable for them. But I've told *Mr Fox* many times to schoolchildren aged between eight and ten and they are always gripped by it. They remember it, too. I've returned to a school a year or two years later and had children come up to me – 'Are you telling that story again? The one about the castle in the wood, and Lady Mary, and the chopped-off hand? I told my brother that story! I told it to my Gran!' In fact the story is easy to retell, with its simple progression from gateway to door, from doorway to stair, from stairway to chamber – and with the repetition and development of memorable phrases. As for what happens, the story might be too strong for young children, except for the fact that it's told twice. The second time they hear about the Bloody Chamber and the severed hand, Lady Mary is in control – and they trust her. In becoming a storyteller, she becomes powerful. She takes charge of her own narrative and turns the tables on the evil Mr Fox.

I love the way Lady Mary is presented in this narrative. Curiosity and suspicion save, rather than endanger her. She's resourceful, brave and intelligent; she rescues herself, and she gets her revenge in one of the neatest reversals of any fairy tale I know.

Reflections on Folk Tales

Do you believe in fairies?

One of the differences between fairy tales and folk tales hinges on the question of belief. Fairy tales don't ask to be believed. The banners of story wave from the top of every fairy-tale tower. No one has ever seriously wondered if the events of Cinderella really happened, or pointed out the ruins of the Sleeping Beauty's castle.

Folk tales, however, do ask for belief – or at least half-belief. They often masquerade as fact, containing information such as the names of people and places which carry a certain amount of conviction. Local pride is often invested in local stories; and if no one has ever believed in a fairy *tale*, lots and lots of people have believed in *fairies* – and in ghosts. Some still do.

William Butler Yeats did. As a boy he walked about Ireland talking to the peasantry and collecting tales; in *The Celtic Twilight*[1] he gives a powerful account of 'an experiment [he] conducted in 1892 with his uncle George Pollexfen and his cousin Lucy Middleton (known in Sligo as a witch) when they

---

1 Yeats, William Butler, *The Celtic Twilight*, 1893, expanded in 1902.

(successfully) summoned the local fairy queen'.[2] Walking at night on the sea shore talking of the fairies, they came to 'a shallow cave amid black rocks' known as the haunt of local fairies. Yeats asked Lucy if she could see anything. The girl stood still, 'and I saw that she was passing into a kind of waking trance, in which the cold sea breeze no longer troubled her, nor the dull boom of the sea . . .' Presently she told Yeats she could hear 'music far inside the rocks, and then a sound of confused talking'. His uncle heard the laughter of unseen children. Lucy next saw a light streaming from the cave, and 'a quantity of little people, dancing'.

> I then bade her call out to the queen of the little people to come and talk with us. There was, however, no answer to her command. I therefore repeated the words myself, and in a moment a very beautiful tall woman came out of the cave. I too had by this time fallen into a kind of trance, in which what we call the unreal had begun to take upon itself a masterful reality, and was able to see the faint gleam of golden ornaments, the shadowy blossom of dim hair.[3]

'*In which what we call the unreal had begun to take upon itself a masterful reality*' – it's a beautiful-sounding thought, if something of an evasion. What does it mean? 'We imagined

---

2 Yeats, W.B., *Writings on Irish Folklore, Legend and Myth*, ed. Robert Welch, xx.

3 Op. cit., 118 et seq.

it so clearly it was almost real?' Yeats next asked the Queen to summon her followers, who appeared, drawing themselves up in four ranks upon the sand; some carrying 'quicken boughs'[4] in their hands, others with 'necklaces made apparently of serpents' scales'. He questioned the Queen about her people, and at last she seemed to lose patience and 'wrote upon the sands – the sands of vision, not the grating sands under our feet – this message for me – "Be careful, and do not seek to know too much about us."' She departed into the cave, and the young girl, Lucy 'awoke out of her trance, and felt again the cold wind of the world, and began to shiver . . . I tell these things as accurately as I can,' Yeats writes, 'and with no theories to blur the record.' And he continues, 'It were as well for us all if we would but raise the cry Lilly the astrologer raised in Windsor Forest, "Regina, Regina Pigmeorum, Veni,"[5] and remember with him, that God visiteth His children in dreams.'

What are we to make of this? Are you, like me, tempted? Do you acknowledge a secret longing to believe? If so, I sympathise. His account is so detailed, so specific – so beautifully written. Would William Butler Yeats lie? Here is the essence of the dilemma: when you know the narrator, the question changes from 'do you believe this story' to 'do you believe this *person*'? Yeats had clearly convinced himself. His younger contemporary Beverley Nichols remembered hearing him exclaim,

> Why can't the English remember that the Irish

---

4 Quickbeam, or rowan.

5 'Come, Queen, Queen of the Little People'.

> people are *Irish*? Why can't they realise that they're dealing with a race of peasants who believe in fairies and are quite right to do so? I myself have seen the saucers of milk which Irish peasants have put outside their doors for the pixies to drink. *If the English could only learn to believe in fairies, there wouldn't ever have been any Irish problem.*[6]

It was all very well for the educated Yeats to indulge in a passionately nationalistic, romantic belief in fairies, to encounter the fairy queen and enjoy the sight of her shadowy hair. For the poor peasantry however, such beliefs could have consequences. In 1821 at Castletown on the Shannon, a woman claimed to have been the subject of a fairy abduction:

> My eldest little boy died, and I was nursing my second, when one night, about Midsummer, as we were sitting at our supper, I was fairy-struck, and fell off my chair. So with that, poor Paddy ran out for one of the neighbours, who desired him send for the priest, which he did to be sure. But when he came he did not know what to do, but said prayers over me, and anointed me for death, and when the holy oil was put on me I was better and continued to mend for several days, but I was still very weak and low; I had . . . a

6 Nichols, Beverley, *The Unforgiving Minute*, 106.

> dimness in my eyes and a ringing in my ears, and my face was greatly altered.[7]

It is a convincing, classic description of a stroke. A few nights later, lying in bed with her husband:

> I heard a great noise, and saw a light in the room. I called Paddy, but he could not hear me. My little child was about three months old and lay asleep by my side. In one minute the house was full of people, men and women, but no one saw them but myself; and one of the women came to the side of the bed and said, 'Judy, get up, you are to come with us; and I will put one in your place to nurse your child.' So with that they dragged me out of bed and put an old woman in my place, who took *my cratur of a child* [creature, a term of endearment] in her arms! I thought I should die, but I could not speak a word. They took me off with them, and there were several horsemen with red caps outside the door, and the women who sat behind them on the horses had blue cloaks. There was a piper on a grey pony that led the way; and when I got to their dwelling I was given a child to nurse. I am not allowed to tell anything that happened when I was there, all I can say is that I never ate one mouthful of their food: if I

---

7 Crofton Croker, Thomas, *Researches in the South of Ireland*, 90.

> did I could never have left them. I came every night to my own house for cold potatoes, and I lived on them. Paddy buried, as he thought, the old woman that was put in my place, but she came away to us. I am twenty years from home, and my husband is married again. This is my son's house. When I came home, Paddy would not own me . . .[8]

Her story seems so full of detail, so full of feeling; it's hard not to be moved by the poignant desperation which drives the stolen woman to creep invisibly back into her own house at nights to eat cold left-over potatoes. She was widely believed in the neighbourhood: but more was going on here than meets the eye. A correspondent of the Irish folklorist Thomas Crofton Croker interviewed the woman in 1821, and explained the background to the tale. Paddy's wife Judy had died (or been stolen by the fairies) in 1800. Her dramatic reappearance took place one night in the winter of 1820. Her husband (or widower, depending on what you believe), had long been re-married, when he and his new wife 'were disturbed by a woman vociferously claiming admission to his cabin and asserting her right to the full and undisturbed sovereignty over the same, in as much as she was the owner's true and lawful wife'.

Imagine it. The confused couple, not knowing what else to do with this strange woman shrieking and beating at the door on a winter's night, let her in. She showed enough knowledge of

---

8 Ibid.

her supposed former husband and his children that they found it difficult to oppose her, and if Paddy didn't recognise his first wife, how should he? She had been gone for twenty years. It was some time before he got up the nerve to throw her out, during which she not only ruled the roost, bossing the second wife about, but paid her way by telling fortunes, a power she claimed the fairies had given her. By the time Crofton Croker's informant spoke with her, she was living with one of Paddy's grown sons, having either convinced him she was his long-dead mother, or perhaps made herself welcome by the money she brought in: the house was 'thronged with visitors, to whom the diviner talked in the common gipsy strain'.

It looks very much as if a travelling fortune-teller, whose existence depended on her quickness to catch hold of details about the people she met, had picked up the tragic tale of Paddy's wife Judy, fairy-struck and conveniently dead for twenty years, and come up with an audacious story, a masterful mix of beliefs about fairies and facts about the household, to obtain for herself not only the shelter of a house over the winter, but huge status in her chosen profession. It worked because everyone 'knew' the story was possible. They believed in fairies.

The exact same belief had terrible consequences in County Tipperary in March 1895, when twenty-six-year-old Bridget Cleary was burned to death by her husband Michael, her own father Patrick, and several other neighbours, because they were convinced she was a fairy substitute and that the true Bridget had been stolen by the fairies of Kylenagranagh Fort, a local fairy hill. A female witness at the trial told how, after burying the body in a field, Michael Cleary had intended to go to the fort on the following Sunday night where he expected to see the true Bridget 'riding on a white horse, and he said he would bring a knife to cut the straps with, and rescue her from the fairies'.[9] Cleary was convicted of manslaughter and sentenced to twenty years penal servitude.

Knowing this, it's difficult not to shiver when Yeats writes approvingly in the 1902 edition of *The Celtic Twilight*: 'Even today our country people speak with the dead and with some who perhaps have never died as we understand death . . .' In his poem *September 1913* he mourns the passing of Ireland's great heroes: 'Romantic Ireland's dead and gone, It's with O'Leary in the grave.' In truth, the romantic vision of Ireland was something he had helped to create.

With every folk tale, with every story, it's worth looking at who is telling it and why. Yeats was an exception: most folklorists do not summon fairy queens or personally believe in the material they collect, and English folklore has never inspired quite such a level of passionate enthusiasm (perhaps because Victorian Englishmen did not feel they had anything much to prove). It's nevertheless interesting to look at two English stories recorded in Thomas Keightley's *The Fairy Mythology* (1828), and look at why and how they were collected. Here's the first tale, which Keightley calls *Addlers and Menters*:[10]

> An old lady in Yorkshire related as follows:– My eldest daughter Betsey was about four years old;

---

9 Bourke, Angela, *The Burning of Bridget Cleary*, 110.
10 Keightley, Thomas, *The Fairy Mythology*, 308 et seq.

I remember it was on a fine summer's afternoon, or rather evening, I was seated in this chair which I now occupy. The child had been in the garden, she came into that entry or passage from the kitchen (on the right side of the entry was the old parlour-door, on the left the door of the common sitting-room; the mother of the child was in a line with both doors); the child, instead of turning towards the sitting room made a pause at the parlour-door, which was open. She stood several minutes quite still; at last I saw her draw her hand quickly towards her body; she set up a loud shriek and ran, or rather flew, to me crying out 'Oh! Mammy, green man will hab me! green man will hab me!'

It was a long time before I could pacify her; I then asked her why she was so frightened. 'O Mammy,' said she, 'all t'parlour is full of *addlers* and *menters*.' Elves and fairies I suppose she meant. She said they were dancing, and a little man in a green coat with a gold-laced cocked hat on his head, offered to take her hand as if he would have her as his partner in the dance.

The mother, upon hearing this, went and looked into the old parlour, but the fairy vision had melted into thin air.

'Such,' adds the narrator, 'is the account I heard of this vision of fairies. The person is still alive who witnessed or supposed she saw it, and

> though a well-informed person, still positively asserts the relations to be strictly true.'*

Keightley's asterisk leads to a cautious, sceptical footnote:

> *And true no doubt it is: ie: the impression made on her imagination was as strong as if the objects had been actually before her. The narrator is the same person who told the preceding boggart story.

An Irishman himself, born 1789 in County Kildare, Thomas Keightley clearly did not believe in fairies. Neither did he collect this story personally. There is a confusion of narrators in *Addlers and Menters*: initially the tale is told by the old lady mentioned in the first sentence, the mother of little Betsey. However, a different voice creeps in to comment upon the layout of the house – the person to whom the old lady is telling the story, whom in the absence of any clue to the contrary, we reasonably suppose must be Keightley himself. In the last paragraph however, we realise that this person is not Keightley, but an unnamed contributor. The story, oddly convincing as it is, comes to us at third hand. How far can we put faith in it?

The detail of the first two paragraphs – the well visualised domestic interior, the little girl coming in from the garden, the pause by the open parlour door, the child's sharply observed gesture of 'drawing her hand quickly towards her body', and her terrified shriek – all suggest a genuine experience of some sort, if only a frightening waking dream or hallucination. *Addlers* and *menters*? Whether dialect words or childish gabble, they somehow carry conviction. But the civilised little man in green coat and gold-laced cocked hat who invites the child to dance – does not. He is hardly convincing as the source of such childish terror. It feels as if this is an anecdote which has been 'finished off' with a conventional literary ending.

The unnamed contributor from whom Keightley collected this tale supplied another story, *The Boggart*. Here it is:

> In the house of an honest farmer in Yorkshire, named George Gilbertson, a Boggart had taken up his abode. He here caused a great deal of annoyance, especially by tormenting the children in various ways. Sometimes their bread and butter would be snatched away, or their porringers of bread and milk be capsised by an invisible hand; for the Boggart never let himself be seen; at other times, the curtains of their beds would be shaken backwards and forwards, or a heavy weight would press on and nearly suffocate them. The parents had often, on hearing their cries, to rush to their aid. There was a kind of closet, formed by a wooden partition, on the kitchen stairs, and a large knot having been driven out of the deal boards of which it was made, there remained a hole. Into this one day the farmer's youngest boy stuck the shoe-horn with which he

was amusing himself, when immediately it was thrown out again, and struck the boy on the head. The agent was of course the Boggart, and it soon became their sport (which they called laking with Boggart) to put the shoe-horn into the hole and have it shot back at them.

The Boggart at length proved such a torment that the farmer and his wife resolved to quit the house and let him have it all to himself. This was put into execution, and the farmer and his family were following the last loads of furniture, when a neighbour named John Marshall came up – 'Well, Georgey,' said he, 'and soa you're leaving t'ould hoose at last?' – 'Heigh, Johnny my lad, I'm forced tull it. For that damned Boggart torments us soa, we can neither rest neet nor day for't, and soa you see, we're forced to flitt.' He scarce had uttered the words when a voice from a deep upright churn cried out, 'Aye, aye, Georgey, we're flitting ye see.' – 'Od damn thee,' cried the poor farmer, 'if I'd known thou'd been there, I wouldn't ha' stirred a peg. Nay nay, it's no use, Mally,' turning to his wife, 'we may as weel turn back again to t'ould hoose as be tormented in another that's not so convenient.'

This tale too seems to have a tacked-on ending. Many readers will recognise the second paragraph as a well-known folk tale type, complete in itself: *Farmer is so bothered by brownie that he decides he must move.*[11] It's different in style from the first paragraph which contains all the specific domestic details. 'Laking with boggart', which means 'playing with the boggart' is convincing Yorkshire usage (they still say 'laiking about' in Yorkshire, and drop the definite article), but the second paragraph is not entirely convincing in its attempt at dialect. Instead of John Marshall's 'Soa you're leaving at last', I'd expect the informal 'Soa th'art leaving at last'. Even if John Marshall is actually addressing George and his family – plural – George responds to him formally 'and soa you see, we're forced to flitt'- instead of the more likely 'and soa tha sees, we're forced to flitt'. The dialogue in the second paragraph of *The Boggart* sounds like what someone *thinks* is the way a Yorkshire farmer talks.

Who was that someone? Was it Keightley himself, or was it his unnamed contributor, the person who listened to the old Yorkshire lady? In another footnote Keightley identifies this person a little further:

> We have abridged this legend from a well-written letter in the Literary Gazette, No. 430 (1825), the writer of which says, he knew the house in which it was said to have occurred.

I went hunting for this letter. It appears in *The Literary Gazette and Journal of Belles Lettres, Arts, Sciences*, the issue for April 16, 1825. The impulse of the anonymous writer is literary and sophisticated. He is responding to an Irish story he had

---

11 Aarne-Thompson Type ML.7020. Motif: F.482.3.1.1.

recently read in Thomas Crofton Croker's *Fairy Legends and Traditions of the South of Ireland*, and he wishes to claim a place for a story local to himself – to record and locate it in the wider context of European folklore.

> Amongst the many traditional legends which its truly amusing compiler [ie: Crofton Croker] has introduced, is one which I considered belonged solely to the neighbourhood of my native village. Indeed I am acquainted with the indentical [*sic*] farmhouse where the mischievous goblin, or, as it is termed in Yorkshire, the Boggart, dislodged by its pranks a farmer and his family. I was surprised to find it a familiar tale with the Irish, and that it is equally well-known in the annals of Danish tradition. My version of the legend runs thus . . .

It's quite clear from this that the letter-writer doesn't believe the Boggart story to be *true*, even though he claims a distant relationship with it: 'An old tailor, whom I but faintly remember, used to say the [shoe]horn was often "pitched" at his head, and at the head of his apprentice, many years after the above circumstance took place . . .' If the letter-writer can only 'faintly' remember the tailor, this tale seems to be an enjoyable piece of local folklore that's been around for a long time. There are details Keightley leaves out:

> As if enraged with these liberties taken with his Boggartship, the goblin commenced a series of

> night persecutions; heavy steps, as of a person in wooden clogs, were often heard clattering down the stairs in the dead hour of darkness; and the pewter and earthen dishes appeared to be dashed on the kitchen floor; though, in the morning, all appeared uninjured on their respective shelves. The children were chiefly marked out as objects of dislike by their unearthly tormentor. The curtains of their beds would be violently pulled backward and forward; anon a heavy weight, as of a human being, would press them nearly to suffocation; they would then scream out for their daddy and mammy, who occupied the adjoining room . . .[12]

The account in the *Literary Gazette* makes better sense than Keightley's abridged version. It's a classic poltergeist tale; the likely culprits are the older boys in a big family, playing tricks and tormenting the younger ones. The *Literary Gazette* version is clear that the shoe-horn projectile was being fired from a large knot-hole in the wooden boards of the cupboard under the stairs, behind which there would have been plenty of room for a boy to hide. Most of the events the narrative describes probably really happened, but were too slight, too inconsequential, to make a good *story*. And so an existing (and excellent) boggart tale gets tacked on to a local incident to provide a satisfying ending.

---

12 Ibid.

The letter-writer certainly doesn't believe the Boggart story. About *Addlers and Menters*, though, he's a lot less sure.

> Mr Croker, who is the author of the amusing volume mentioned above, says that fairies have not been seen for many years in the North of England. I can inform him, if not in the memory of man, they have been seen in the memory of woman, in a village in the East Riding of Yorkshire. A respectable female, who is nearly [i.e.: closely] related to the writer of this, and who is now alive, beheld, when she was a little girl, a troop of fairies 'deftly footing a roundel daunce' in her mother's large old wainscoted parlour . . . I have frequently heard it related by her venerable mother, and subsequently by herself. I shall give the tale as I received it from the old lady.[13]

This is a family story, told first-hand to the narrator – which explains its sharply focussed immediacy. We can be pretty sure that whatever little Betsey saw or thought she saw, the words given to her are exactly what she said. 'Addlers and menters'? No one would make that up. The words aren't dialect: even her mother wasn't sure what they meant. 'Oh mammy, green man will hab me, green man will hab me!' That sounds true too. But could she really have come up with the description of the courteous little man in a green coat with

---

13 Op. cit.

a gold-laced cocked hat who gestured for her to join in a dance?

Gold-laced cocked hats were high fashion in the first quarter of the eighteenth century, along with powdered wigs. They came briefly back in 1775 and then disappeared for ever with the French revolution. In 1825, the year this account was published, an 'old' lady might have been sixty. If she was twenty-five when little Betsey was four, the events in *Addlers and Menters* would have taken place around 1795. It's most unlikely a four-year-old child in a Yorkshire village would ever have seen a gold-laced cocked hat.[14] Much more likely, this detail was suggested to her by her mother in the course of repeated questionings and retellings of the troubling incident. For troubling it was. You can hear the uncertainty in the letter-writer's voice; 'Such is the account I heard of this vision of fairies; the person is still alive who witnessed, or supposed she saw it, and though a well-informed person, still positively asserts the relation to be strictly true.' It's the dilemma of belief again: he *knows* this lady, she is his relative. She is positive about what she saw, and her mother witnessed her reaction to the event. *Something* happened. Can he disbelieve her? And he wants to believe her – doesn't he? Just as Yeats wanted to believe in the fairy queen and I want to believe in Yeats.

There's something terribly convincing about the very

---

14 'Gold-laced hats were again general in [17]75 and in 78 were adopted by many to give them a military air . . . [but] the French revolution, in 1789, completed the downfall of the three-cornered cocked hat on both sides of the channel.' James Robinson Planché, *History of British Costume*, London 1836.

inconsequentiality of 'true' stories – also known as folk tales. You have a child screaming, 'Green man will hab me!' and talking spooky nonsense about addlers and menters, and prickles will be running down your own spine. I have a feeling that the little girl's mother invented the courtly little green man in order to make the child's vision less terrifying. 'A green man, darling? Oh, a lovely little fairy man in a gold-laced hat! He didn't mean to frighten you. He only wanted to ask you to dance!' And such is the power of motherly suggestion, the child soon agrees that's what she saw. The mother has made it into a *story*, turned an unsettling, frightening moment into a comfortable narrative.

A story is something constructed, something we know is 'made up'. A story makes sense. By contrast, most 'true' ghost stories are distressingly pointless, such as that of the modern phantom who keeps appearing on the A38 near Wellington.[15] He stands in the middle of the road flashing a torch, and appears to be looking for something on the ground, much to the alarm of motorists who have to swerve or brake for him. And that's it. There's no more. No explanation. It's not a story, it's a happening.

And that's the reason people believe it. Human beings are prepared to believe or to half-believe anecdotes about ghosts, fairies and UFOs almost in an inverse relation to how much sense they make.

We believe them because we don't think anyone would make them up.

We believe them precisely because they're not *stories* at all.

---

15 Ackroyd, Peter, 'The Phantom of the A38', *The English Ghost*, 105.

White Ladies

In my book *Dark Angels* the fictitious twelfth-century castle of La Motte Rouge in the Welsh Marches is haunted by a mournful White Lady who wanders the courtyard on dark, misty nights, wringing her hands and moaning softly. She's creepy but harmless, she's forgotten her own name, she is the diminished pagan spirit of the spring which feeds the castle's cistern and she is older, much older, than the castle in which she is now contained. The various Christian inhabitants now regard her with attitudes ranging from fear to pity. In this shortened extract my young hero, Wolf, encounters her late one night:

> In the faint moonlight Wolf could see the yard – an expanse of greyish mud. He hurried across, and was about to slip around the corner of the Hall, where the huddled buildings made a darkness as intense as ink – when instinct made him pause, and a woman stepped around the corner from the opposite direction. She saw him, and held up a warning finger . . . She was wrapped in flimsy

clothing for this time of night: fluttering white garments with a light veil pulled across her face. She must be a lady of the household, one of Lady Agnes' women, though he hadn't noticed anyone like her at supper. Mist blew around her as she swayed towards him and murmured in a melancholy, musical voice, '*Dewi methu mynd i mewn.*'

'I'm sorry, I don't speak Welsh . . .'

Plainly disapproving of his ignorance, the lady shook her head sadly. After a moment she tried again, in the same mournful voice, but this time in Latin. Her accent was strange, but Wolf understood her. 'I can't get in,' she said softly, clasping her hands.

'You can't get in? You mean, into the chapel?'

'I can't get in.'

. . . Wolf paused. Perhaps she was mad. Through the transparent veil he glimpsed a sweet, wild face. 'What's your name, lady?' he asked gently. But the question seemed to distress her. 'I can't remember,' she moaned, swaying in a sort of absent-minded dance. '*Gwae fi!* I can't remember!'

Wolf stared at her feet. She had crossed that dirty yard right behind him. His own shoes were clotted with mud. Yet there wasn't a single stain on her little white slippers.'[1]

---

1 Langrish, Katherine, *Dark Angels*, 78/9.

White Ladies are different from other ghosts. They sometimes inspire terror, but the feeling most often associated with them is a tingle of eerie sadness. It is this sensation Wilkie Collins evokes in *The Woman in White*[2] as the young hero Walter Hartright walks home at dead of night along the deserted road from Hampstead to London, when

> in one moment, every drop of blood in my body was brought to a stop by the touch of a hand laid lightly and suddenly on my shoulder from behind. I turned on the instant, with my fingers tightening round the handle of my stick.
>
> There, in the middle of the broad, bright high-road – there, as if it had that moment sprung out of the earth or dropped from heaven – stood the figure of a solitary Woman, dressed from head to foot in white garments, her face bent in grave inquiry on mine, her hand pointing to the black cloud over London, as I faced her.[3]

Traditional ghost stories often come complete with 'explanations' for the apparition which involve some sort of crime: the ghost is unable to rest because it is either the victim or the perpetrator. White Ladies are often described as murdered brides or sweethearts, or girls who have drowned themselves for love: they are frequently associated with water.

---

2 Though the eponymous woman is not actually a ghost.

3 Collins, Wilkie, *The Woman in White*, ch. IV.

A story from Yorkshire, reported in 1823, tells how a maiden robed in white may be seen on Hallowe'en at the spot where the rivers Hodge and Dove meet, standing with her golden hair streaming and her arm around the neck of a white doe. From Somerset, Ruth Tongue describes three charming apparitions:

> One of them is the White Lady of Wellow, who haunts St Julian's Well, now in a cottage garden. She played the part of a banshee to the Lords of Hungerford, but she seems to have been a well spirit rather than a ghost. The Lake Lady of Orchardleigh is another white lady who is rather a fairy than a ghost. But the most fairy-like of the three is the White Rider of Corfe, who . . . gallops along the road on a white horse, turns clean aside by a field gate and into the middle of a meadow, where she vanishes. I was told about her by some old-age pensioners in the Blackdown Hills in 1946. One of them said, 'She shone like a dewdrop,' and another of them, 'T'was like liddle bells all a-chime.'[4]

In Wales it seems there are two varieties of White Ladies, the *Dynes Mewn Gwyn* and the *ladi wen*: the first is a true ghost; the second an apparition which haunts the place where someone has died a violent death. Not all White Ladies are harmless. Jane C. Beck tells of one which appeared at Ogmore Castle

---

4 Tongue, Ruth & Briggs, Katharine, *Somerset Folklore*, 120.

near Bridgend, Glamorgan, where she was believed to guard a treasure under the tower floor. One man was brave enough to speak to her; she gave permission to take half the treasure and showed him where it lay, but when he was so greedy as to return for the rest:

> The White Lady then set upon him, and to his dismay, he found she had claws instead of fingers, and with these she nearly tore him to pieces.[5]

In his *Teutonic Mythology*, Jacob Grimm recounts many tales of White Ladies who haunt mountainsides, some of whom actually appear by day:

> In the Otomannsberg near Geismar village, a fire is said to burn at night. Every seven years there comes out a maiden in snowy garments, holding a bunch of keys in her hand. Another white woman with a bunch of keys appears on the castle-rock at Baden at the hour of noon . . . At Osterode, every Easter Sunday before sunrise, may be seen a white maiden, who slowly walks down to the brook, and there washes; a large bunch of keys hangs at her girdle . . .[6]

To those who encounter them and act with courtesy, these

---

5 Beck, Jane C., 'The White Lady of Britain and Ireland', *Folklore Vol 81*, 1970, 297.

6 Grimm, Jacob, *Teutonic Mythology*, Vol. III, 962–3.

White Ladies sometimes give apparently trivial gifts – hair-combings or flax seeds – which later turn into gold. But they can also be scary, such as the white woman who comes to wail at the bedside of a traveller in a lonely hunting lodge, her appearance heralded by a 'scuffing of shoes'. Sometimes they have goats' feet, or long claw-like fingernails. Occasionally they spin as they walk, and some spin gold. Often they are the guardians of treasure hoards. Grimm finds in these legends the attributes of Teutonic goddesses:

> For the origin of these White Women we need not go to the Celtic *matrons* and *fays*, who are closely related to them; our own antiquity brings us to beings nearer still. Elfins and swan-wives appear in white shining garments; among goddesses may be named three in particular, of whom the '*white woman*' and finally the '*nun*' might be the outcome: *Holda*, who in the very same way combs and bathes in the midday sun, *Berhta*, white by her very name, who spins and weaves, *Ostara*, to whom the people offered up may-lilies. Holda and Berhta bestow trifling gifts, which turn into gold . . . Berhta as the white ancestress appears when a death is at hand; so does the white maid . . .[7]

Perchta or Berhta was concerned with household tasks,

7 Grimm, Jacob, *Teutonic Mythology*, 968.

especially spinning, and she punished lazy spinners by tangling and befouling their flax. She could be gracious and benevolent, but had a dark side too, blinding, or ripping open with her long fingernails those who offended her. Despite this aspect, Grimm explains that the name Berhta means white or bright, and that as a White Lady she was considered a kindly, family ghost:

> The white lady, by her very name, has altogether the same meaning, for *peraht*, *berht* or *brecht*, signifies bright, light, white. This white lady usually attaches herself to particular families, but even then she usually keeps the name of Berta, e.g.: Berta of Rosenberg. In snow-white garments she shows herself by night in princely houses, she rocks or dandles the babies, while their nurses sleep: she acts as the old grandmother or ancestress of the family.[8]

I'm strongly reminded of little Princess Irene's great-great (ever-so-many-greats) grandmother in George MacDonald's *The Princess and the Goblin*, a beautiful woman with long white hair who can seem both old and young, who inhabits the top floor of the castle tower, and sits spinning her magical moony wheel. Little Irene must climb the dark tower steps to find her:

> When she reached the top she stood a moment

8 Op. cit., 280.

> listening in the dark, for there was no moon there. Yes! it was! it was the hum of the spinning wheel! What a diligent grandmother, to work both day and night! She tapped gently at the door.
>
> 'Come in, Irene,' said the sweet voice.
>
> The princess opened the door and entered. There was the moonlight streaming in at the window, and in the middle of the moonlight sat the old lady in her black dress with the white lace, and her silvery hair mingling with the moonlight, so that you could not have told which was which.[9]

In France, White Ladies are known as the Dames Blanches. According to Thomas Keightley, they lurk in narrow places such as 'ravines, fords and rivers' where those on foot are unable to avoid them. 'The Dame Blanche sometimes requires him who she thus meets to join her in a dance, or hand her over [ie: assist her to cross] a plank. If he does, she makes him many courtesies, and then vanishes.'[10] If he refused, however, she would throw him into the ditch. A Dame Blanche used to sit on a narrow wooden bridge, the Pont d'Angot over the Dive, in Falaise, and would not let anyone pass unless they kneeled down before her. It sounds very much like some old tradition of paying reverence to the spirit of the river.

And what of the Lady of the Lake, in Malory's *Le Morte*

---

9 MacDonald, George, *The Princess and the Goblin*, ch. 11.
10 *The Fairy Mythology*, ed. Thomas Keightley, 474.

D'Arthur? Is she a White Lady? She is seen by Arthur and Merlin 'going upon the lake', and although it is not actually her arm 'clothed in white samite' which brandishes the sword Excalibur above the water, she informs Arthur that the sword is her own.[11] Whose is the arm, then? We are never told. Along with other ancient peoples, the British worshipped deities, many or mainly female – of rivers, streams and springs. Most of their names are forgotten, but we still know Sabrina of the Severn, and Sulis of Aquae Sulis, the hot springs at Bath. Into the waters of these springs and rivers offerings were thrown, just as we still throw coins into fountains, and many is the bronze- or iron-age sword which has been recovered from river beds and marshlands. How many Bediveres have thrown precious weapons to the Lady of the Lake? And what did they hope to receive in return? Health? Wealth? Victory?

In John Masefield's magical, wintry book *The Box of Delights*, there's a passage which well combines the ambiguous mystery and dread of the White Lady. Kay Harker is out on the Roman Road on a night 'as black as a pocket' and sees something white moving towards him.

> He remembered, that Cook had said, there was a White Lady who 'walked' out Duke's Brook way. This thing that was coming was a White Lady . . . but supposing it was a White Wolf, standing on its hind legs and ready to pounce. It looked like a wolf; its teeth were gleaming. Then the moon

---

11 Malory, Thomas, *Le Morte d'Arthur*, Book I, ch 25.

> shone out again; he saw that it was a White Lady who held her hand in a peculiar way, so that he could see a large ring, with a glittering 'longways cross' on it . . .
>
> 'Come Kay,' she said, 'you must not stay here; the Wolves are running: listen.'[12]

Significantly the White Lady (in this case wholly benevolent) is believed by Cook to haunt a water course, Duke's Brook. John Masefield's fiction is full of folklore, in which he clearly took great delight: his White Lady runs true to type. The Irish or Scottish banshee is also associated with water, as is the Washer at the Ford who presages the death of Cú Chulainn:

> [A] young girl, thin and white-skinned and having yellow hair, washing and ever washing, and wringing out clothing that was all stained crimson red, and she crying and keening all the time.[13]

In later Irish tradition 'the Banshee or White Fairy, sometimes called She Frogh or House Fairy' is described as 'a small shrivelled old woman with long white hair'.[14] These titles, 'White Fairy' or 'House Fairy', take us back to the goddess

---

12 Masefield, John, *The Box of Delights*, ch VI, 165.
13 Gregory, Lady Augusta, *Cuchulain of Muirthemne*, 335.
14 Crofton Croker, Thomas, *Researches in the South of Ireland*, 91.

Berhte again, with her role as supernatural housekeeper, ancestress, guardian of keys, overseer of propriety. That formidable collector of folk tales, the Reverend Sabine Baring-Gould, tells two stories of a White Lady who was his own ancestress, his great-great grandmother Madame Gould of Lew Trenchard, Devon. In 1832, Baring-Gould's grandfather employed a carpenter to renovate the church at Lew Trenchard. The curious carpenter opened the vault of this 'notable woman':

> It was night, and he had his lantern. I tell the tale as he told it me. When he opened her coffin she sat up, and a light streamed from her above that of his lantern. He was so panic-stricken that he fled the church, and ran home a distance of a quarter of a mile. And as he told me, she followed him, and he knew that, because his shadow went before him the whole way.[15]

That's not enough by itself to make a White Lady out of Madame Gould, but the next tale does: in April 1795 a young man of the parish returned home to Lew Trenchard after living in America for some years. Riding through the Lew Valley on a moonlit night,

> [H]e looked into a newly ploughed field, in which a plough had been left. On this was seated a lady in white satin, with long hair floating over

---

15 Baring-Gould, Sabine, *A Book of Folk-Lore*, 33.

> her shoulders. Her face was uplifted and her eyes directed towards the moon, so that he had a full view of it. He recognised her at once as Madame Gould, and, taking off his hat, called out, 'I wish you a very good night, Madame.' She bowed in return, and waved her hand. The man noticed the sparkle of her diamond rings as she did so. On reaching home, after the first greetings . . . he said to his relatives, 'What do you think? I have seen the strange Madame Gould sitting on a plough, at this time of night, looking at the moon.' All those who heard it stared . . .
>
> 'Madame,' said they, 'was buried seven days ago in Lew Church.'
>
> . . . Now, the remarkable point in this story, which I heard from the family is that Madame was seated on a plough, and the plough was the symbol of Frî. I have troubled the reader with this story only because I think the incident of sitting on the plough is important as connecting the White Lady of Lew Trenchard with Frî, the Anglo-Saxon goddess.[16]

Not much is known of the Anglo-Saxon Frî or Frig, from whom we derive the name of Friday, but she probably shares the

16 Baring-Gould, Sabine, *A Book of Folk-Lore*, 80.

attributes of the Norse goddesses Frigg, associated with wealth, childbirth, and power over the household, and Freyja (the name simply means 'lady') associated with fertility and crops. Folk belief said it was dangerous to leave a plough outside, for if Freyja sat on it, it would no longer be of use. Baring-Gould adds that he believes the Lew Trenchard tradition to be older than this story. 'It attached itself first to a certain Susannah Gould' who was married in 1729 to Peter Truscott, son of the rector of the parish at that time, and who 'died on her way back from church, in her white wedding garments, and was buried four days later. Such a striking event naturally provoked attention, and the earlier tradition of a White Lady at once adhered to her, and clung to her till some sixty-six years later, when it . . . attached itself to another notable lady of the same family.'[17]

This handing down of the role of White Lady from generation to generation is a striking feature of the story, and once again we see that the only safe way to behave to her is with courtesy! Like little Princess Irene's beautiful grandmother, Lew Trenchard's White Lady seems to act as tutelary deity or family guardian. It seems clear that as Jane Beck says, 'The modern day ghost known as the White Lady is . . . [a] creature with a heritage reaching back to the darkest recesses of time. Although her most usual form today is that of a gliding spectre, some of the acts she performs recall her earlier condition as a deity.'[18]

---

17 Ibid.

18 Beck, Jane C., *The White Lady of Britain and Ireland*, Folklore Vol 81, 1970, 292–3.

Whatever their history, I like White Ladies – beautiful, eerie creatures draped in moonlight, trailing clouds of grief and longing for those far-away ages when they still had the power to bless – or to curse.

Wise fools and simpletons

There are fools. There are foolish fools, and there are wise fools. Foolish fools, in the oral tradition and in literature, are simpletons. They make bad decisions. Granted three wishes, they squander their chances, wish for something as modest as a black pudding, wish it on to their partner's nose during a marital squabble, and use up the third wish to remove it again. Stories about them are intended as laughter-provoking demonstrations of how *not* to behave, yet sometimes they throw light upon the unsuspected absurdities of worldly wisdom. Wise fools on the other hand are often conscious critics, iconoclasts who from a theoretically lowly but in fact often privileged social position, turn their wit upon their masters.

Perhaps ever since there have been rulers, there have been professional fools, jesters and comedians who have been given (or who have taken) licence to expose and hold up to ridicule the kings, priests, presidents and public figures, the laws, mores, prejudices, injustices and – yes – follies of the societies in which they live. They are a world-wide phenomenon. In her book *Fools Are Everywhere*, Beatrice K. Otto chronicles court jesters not only all over Europe, but also in Russia, India, and Imperial China. All employed the same kind of impudence, requiring quick wits, strong nerves and a clever tongue. She quotes Marais, jester to Louis XIII, remarking to his king:

> 'There are two things about your job I couldn't cope with – eating alone and shitting in company.' ('Il y a deux choses dans votre métier dont je ne me pourrais accommoder . . . De manger tout seul et de chier en compagnie.')[1]

Marais strikes home to a truth about the surreal world of the court. Cocooned in stultifying ceremony, kings found relief in the direct, disrespectful speech of their jesters – the only members of court who were allowed to speak to them man to man. Like the child in *The Emperor's New Clothes*, Marais sees through the apparent splendour of Louis's life, and acknowledges it as both lonely and bizarre. When Henry VIII of England was given the title 'Defender of the Faith,' one of his jesters is reported to have shaken his head and said to Henry (using the familiar, informal, mode of address), 'Let thou and I defend one another, and let faith alone to defend itself.' In both instances the role of jester or fool echoes that of the slave who would stand in the triumphal car directly behind a victorious Roman general, and whisper in his ear from time to time, 'Remember, thou art mortal.' The work of these jesters

---

1 Otto, Beatrice K., *Fools Are Everywhere*, 48.

is as much to keep the monarch grounded – even sane – as it is to keep him amused.

And a wise ruler would listen to what his fool told him. Shakespeare's *King Lear* is a play which examines folly and madness as closely as it does pride and ingratitude. Lear's folly is to relinquish power and divide his kingdom between his two elder daughters. It's Lear's fool who stays with him when everyone else has left him. And the fool gives good advice, as fools will:

> Fool: Canst tell how an oyster makes his shell?
> Lear: No.
> Fool: Nor I neither; but I can tell why a snail has a house.
> Lear: Why?
> Fool: Why, to put his head in, not to give it away to his daughter and leave his horns without a case . . . If thou wert my fool, nuncle, I'd have thee beaten for being old before thy time.
> Lear: How's that?
> Fool: Thou shouldst not have been old before thou wert wise.[2]

It is the Fool's privilege to speak the bare truth with a degree of safety. Erasmus, in his 1509 essay *The Praise of Folly*, places in

2 *King Lear*, I, vi.

the mouth of the goddess Folly all sorts of criticisms of society and the church which if he hadn't been able to present the book as a brilliant *jeu d'esprit* (it made Pope Leo X laugh), might well have got him into trouble. In this passage he comments on the folly of scholars who even ask, let alone answer, some of the burning questions of the day:

> The primitive disciples were very frequent in administering the holy sacrament, breaking bread from house to house; yet should they be asked . . . the nature of transubstantiation? the possibility of one body being in several different places at the same time? the difference betwixt the several aspects of Christ in heaven on the cross, and in the consecrated bread? what time is required for the transubstantiating of the bread into flesh? how it can be done by a short sentence pronounced by the priest . . . were they asked, I say, these and several other confused enquiries, I do not believe they could answer so readily as our mincing school-men now-a-days take pride in doing.[3]

These were dangerous speculations: yet Erasmus could point out that he had placed these words in the mouth of Folly herself.

We live dangerously when we laugh at a jester or a live

3 Erasmus, Desiderius, *The Praise of Folly*, 214.

comedian. We know it's not safe to sit in the front row: we know that he or she has a mastery of words and is likely to get the better of us if we cross verbal swords. But the jester, dependent on his nimble wits, is only one type of wise fool. There is another type of folly, the folly of the simpleton.

Simpletons pose no such danger to the bystander. (If you're thinking we're all too civilised now to laugh at 'the village idiot', stop for a moment to consider what that laughter consisted of. Didn't it – doesn't it – consist of finding ignorance funny? Social ignorance, lack of *nous* – ignorance of 'the way things are done'? Is such laughter dead?)

Stories about simpletons often end with the lucky fool coming up smelling of roses. *Jack and the Beanstalk* is one of the best known examples. There are a number of different versions of this traditional tale, but in every one of them Jack is such a simpleton, such a fool, that he sells his mother's cow for a handful of beans which (after his angry mother has hurled them into the garden) grow up into a beanstalk that touches the clouds.

> As he was going along, he met a butcher, who enquired why he was driving the cow from home? Jack replied, it was his intention to sell it. The butcher held some curious beans in his hat; they were of various colours, and attracted Jack's notice: this did not pass unnoticed by the butcher, who, knowing Jack's easy temper, thought now was the time to take advantage of it, and . . . asked what was the price of the cow, offering at

> the same time all the beans in his hat for her. The silly boy could not [enough] express his pleasure at what he supposed so great an offer: the bargain was struck instantly and the cow exchanged for a few paltry beans.

This is one of the earliest printed versions of the tale, published by Benjamin Tabart in 1807 and, according to Iona and Peter Opie, 'the source of all substantial retellings of the story'.[4] It is a highly literary version which includes a long, dull, moralistic piece of back-story intended to make readers feel Jack is justified in stealing from the Giant. Tabart also explains away Jack's stupidity in accepting the beans: it was due to the magical influence of a fairy who wished to benefit him. Over eighty years later, Joseph Jacobs similarly attempts to dilute Jack's folly: on meeting a 'queer little old man' who offers him five beans for his cow, Milky-White, Jack replies with sarcasm: '"Go along," says Jack; "wouldn't you like it?"'[5] and the old man has actually to *explain* to him that the beans are magic and will 'grow right up to the sky' before Jack will accept the bargain.

It looks as though both Tabart and Jacobs found the traditional Jack too foolish to be attractive as a hero. And yet his folly is more than half the point. It is telling that these literary additions haven't survived very well; they haven't 'stuck' to the story. Most of us remember Jack as a simpleton who is

---

4 Opie, Iona and Peter, 'The History of Jack and the Bean-Stalk', *The Classic Fairy Tales*, 212.

5 Jacobs, Joseph, 'Jack and the Beanstalk', *English Fairy Tales*, 60.

cheated out of his valuable cow for a handful of apparently worthless beans. It's as if the beans gain their magical properties *in response to* the innocence and folly of the hero. Ultimately Jack wins and the trickster is the loser. And the lesson which the tale preaches is that sharp practice doesn't always pay and that good fortune watches over the innocent and trustful.

This is a lesson repeated over and over in fairy tales. Usually it's the third son, the young, slightly stupid one, whose innocence gives him the edge over his more worldly elder brothers.

> There was a man who had three sons, the youngest of whom was called Dummling [Simpleton], and was despised, mocked and sneered at on every occasion.
>
> It happened that the eldest wanted to go into the forest to hew wood, and before he went his mother gave him a beautiful sweet cake and a bottle of wine in order that he might not suffer from hunger or thirst.
>
> When he entered the forest he met a little grey-haired old man who bade him good-day and said, 'Do give me a piece of cake out of your pocket, and let me have a draught of your wine; I am so hungry and thirsty.' But the clever son answered, 'If I give you my cake and wine, I shall have none for myself: be off with you.'[6]

---

6 'The Golden Goose', KHM 64, *Grimm's Fairy Tales*, 322.

Is the clever son really so very clever? We listeners, we readers, we know how these things go. Not so clever after all. For:

> when he began to hew down a tree, it was not long before he made a false stroke, and the axe cut him in the arm, so he had to go home and have it bound up. And this was the little grey man's doing.[7]

Soon it's the second son's turn. Characterised as 'sensible', he fares no better, and then it is Dummling's chance. His mother gives him 'a cake made with water and baked in the cinders, and a bottle of sour beer'; but when the little grey man appears, Dummling readily agrees to share his food,

> and when he pulled out his cinder-cake, it was a fine sweet cake, and the sour beer had become good wine. So they ate and drank, and after that the little man said, 'Since you have a good heart and are willing to divide what you have, I will give you good luck. There stands an old tree, cut it down, and you will find something at the roots.' Then the little old man took leave of him.
>
> Dummling went and cut down the tree, and when it fell there was a goose sitting in the roots with feathers of pure gold.[8]

---

7 Ibid.
8 Ibid.

This is not the goose that lays the golden eggs, but its pure gold feathers attract the attention of an innkeeper's greedy daughter who tries to pull out one of its feathers. The moment she touches it, she sticks fast. Her sisters soon follow suit, and soon Dummling has a whole tail of people running after him willy-nilly. Dummling is innocent of greed, and that is why he is fit to own the golden goose. People who covet wealth, this story says, are forced to run after it, become literally stuck to it in an undignified straggle: whereas Dummling, who shared the little he had, is worthy to marry the King's daughter.

Sometimes stories about simpletons set out simply to amuse the listeners with catalogues of extravagant folly. In Joseph Jacobs' *The Three Sillies*, a father, mother and daughter allow beer to run all over the cellar floor while they sit weeping over improbable catastrophes:

> 'Oh!' says the father, 'Look at that horrid mallet! Suppose you and our daughter was to be married, and was to have a son, and he was to grow up, and was come down into the cellar to draw the beer, and the mallet was to fall on his head and kill him!'[9]

The visiting gentleman promises to marry the daughter if he can find three people sillier than she is – and he succeeds, so this tale too has a happy conclusion. (La Fontaine's fable *The*

---

9 Jacobs, Joseph, 'The Three Sillies', *English Fairy Tales*, 11.

Milkmaid and her Pail[10] warns against the opposite danger of building castles in the air and counting chickens before they are hatched.) In this way, even foolish fools may provide object lessons. In *Frederick and Catherine*, simple Catherine ricochets from one domestic disaster to another:

> At midday home came Frederick: 'Now wife, what have you ready for me?' 'Ah, Freddy,' she answered, 'I was frying a sausage for you, but whilst I was drawing the beer to drink with it, the dog took it away out of the pan, and whilst I was running after the dog, all the beer ran out, and whilst I was drying up the beer with the flour, I knocked over the can as well, but be easy, the cellar is quite dry again.'[11]

In spite of the disasters she causes, the utterly incompetent Catherine is always good tempered. Nothing upsets her, and this is true too of stories such as *Hans In Luck*, in which a young man trades away seven years' wages on his journey home, delighted with each successive bad bargain, till he is left with nothing but two stones. When the heavy stones fall into a well and he is left with nothing, he thanks God for his good fortune in not having to carry them any more:

> 'There is no man under the sun so fortunate as

10 La Fontaine, Jean de, 'La Laitière et le Pot au Lait', *Fables*, VII, 10, 301.

11 'Frederick and Catherine', KHM 59, *Grimm's Fairy Tales*, 284.

> I,' he cried out. With a light heart and free from every burden he now ran on until he was with his mother at home.[12]

The happiness of such characters may pose a sly challenge to our own material values.

Some tales involve entire villages of fools: people have always enjoyed poking fun at their neighbours, as borne out by the old saying, 'Yorkshire born and Yorkshire bred, Strong in the arm and thick in the head'. (I'm from Yorkshire. Insert any place-name you like that scans.) Typical of such stories is this one:

> The men of Austwick in Yorkshire had only one knife between them, so they had a habit of keeping it always under one tree when it was not in use. If it was not there when it was wanted, the man needing it called out, 'Whittle to the tree!' The plan worked well until one day a party of labourers took it to a neighbouring moor to cut their bread and cheese. At the day's end they decided to leave the knife there for the next day, and to mark the place where it lay they stuck it into the ground in the shadow of a great black cloud. But the next day the cloud was gone, and so was the whittle, and they never saw it again.[13]

---

12 'Hans in Luck', KHM 83, *Grimm's Fairy Tales*, 386.

13 Briggs, Katherine, 'Whittle to the Tree', *A Dictionary of British Folk-tales*, Part A, Vol 2, 348.

At least one tale slyly suggests there may sometimes be method in this kind of madness. It recounts a stratagem of the villagers of Gotham who had prevented King John from travelling over their meadows, since they believed any ground over which a king passed would thereafter become a public road (the king's highway). The angry king sends messengers to punish their incivility, but:

> The villagers . . . thought of an expedient to turn away his Majesty's displeasure . . . When the messengers arrived at Gotham, they found some of the inhabitants endeavouring to drown an eel in a pool of water; some were employed in dragging carts upon a large barn, to shade the wood from the sun; others were tumbling their cheeses down a hill . . . and some were employed in hedging in a cuckoo . . . in short, they were all employed in some foolish way or other, which convinced the king's servants that it was a village of fools, whence arose the old adage, 'the wise men', or the 'The fools of Gotham'![14]

Folly may be wisdom, cloaked. This story, as so often with stories about fools, asks us to dig deep, not to accept things at face value. In the following exchange Shakespeare's fool

---

14 Briggs, Katharine, 'The Wise Men of Gotham', *A Dictionary of British Folk-tales,* Part A, Vol 2, 349.

Feste demonstrates the folly of his mistress the Lady Olivia:

> Feste: Good madonna, why mournest thou?
> Olivia: Good fool, for my brother's death.
> Feste: I think his soul is in hell, madonna.
> Olivia: I know his soul is in heaven, fool.
> Feste: The more fool, madonna, to mourn for your brother's soul, being in heaven. Take away the fool, gentlemen.[15]

By this neat Socratic sleight-of-hand he also demonstrates the limitations of both philosophy and religion, applied to the human condition. For we know very well how quickly these structures can crumble under the shockwave of grief. As a believing Christian, Olivia ought not to mourn her brother who is now in heaven. Logically, she should rejoice. But grief doesn't work like that and Feste knows it. On the other hand, almost a year after her brother's death perhaps it *is* time Olivia was teased or prodded out of what threatens literally to become a habit of over-the-top mourning:

> The element itself till seven years heat
> Shall not behold her face at ample view,
> But like a cloistress she will veiled walk
> And water once a day her chamber round
> With eye-offending brine.[16]

---

15 *Twelfth Night*, I, v.
16 Op. cit., I, i.

Feste's fool's wisdom, his logical-illogical wisecracking, begins the process which will finally release Olivia from her shroud of grief. She will fall in love and life will go on.

'We are fools for Christ's sake,' says St Paul,[17] and again: 'the message of the cross is foolishness to those who are perishing, but to us who are being saved it is the power of God.'[18] Perhaps this echoes Christ's message, 'Suffer the little children to come unto me and forbid them not: for of such is the kingdom of God. Whosoever shall not receive the kingdom of God as a little child, he shall not enter heaven.'[19] As jesters resemble children in their undeceived clear-sightedness, so simpletons resemble children in their simplicity and innocence. In *The Little Flowers of Saint Francis of Assisi*, a fourteenth-century compilation of tales about the saint and his brother Franciscans, there is a character called Brother Juniper: a complete dolt who might have walked straight out of *The Wise Men of Gotham* or *Frederick and Catherine*. Like Catherine, he is utterly literal in his application of requests and commands – to a truly unsettling extent.

> On a time at Saint Mary of the Angels, when all afire with the love of God he was visiting a sick brother, he asked him with much compassion: 'Can I do thee any service?' Replied the sick man: 'Much comfort would it give me, if thou couldest get me a pig's trotter to eat.' Straightway cried

17 1 Corinthians 4:10.
18 1 Corinthians 1:18.
19 Mark 10:14–15.

> Brother Juniper, 'Leave that to me, I'll fetch you one at once!'[20]

Brother Juniper hurries off into the forest with a knife, finds a herd of pigs, cuts off a foot from one of them and runs away with it to prepare and cook it for the sick man. The swineherd follows and complains of his action to Saint Francis, who berates Brother Juniper: 'O Brother Juniper, why hast thou now given this great scandal?'

> Brother Juniper . . . was amazed, being surprised that any one should be angry at so charitable a deed: for it seemed to him that these temporal things were nought, save in so far as men of their charity shared them with their neighbours. And Brother Juniper answered: 'Doubt not, my Father, that I will pacify him straightway and content him. And why should he be so disquieted, seeing that this pig, whose foot I have cut off, was rather God's than his, and great charity has been done thereby?'[21]

Needless to say the swineherd is not pacified at all, but 'exceeding wroth'. We miss the point here, however, if our only response is to wince on behalf of the pig. The Franciscan view of animals was a religious, not a sentimental one, and animal

---

20 *The Little Flowers of Saint Francis of Assisi*, 221.
21 Op. cit., 223–4.

rights lay a long, long way in the future. Whoever wrote this fable down fully expected the contemporary reader to regard Brother Juniper's action as great folly (you don't mutilate live pigs) and to understand St Francis's anger. And *yet* we are asked to see his folly as saintly, to put aside our usual habits and enter a mind-set which quite simply views all things – everything – as belonging already to God. 'He would be a good Friar,' said St Francis, 'who had overcome the world as perfectly as Brother Juniper'. Brother Juniper's single-minded concentration on God is at once ridiculous, frightening – and holy. Fools and saints *are* rather frightening. They don't operate by the normal rules. When we look at their actions, we are sometimes startled into questioning our own. And this has been the purpose of fools down the ages – holding up the glass of folly to what we think is wisdom. Are you a fool? Am I?

> Lear: Dost thou call me a fool, boy?
>
> Fool: All thy other titles thou hast given away. That, thou wast born with.[22]

22 *King Lear*, I, iv.

Water spirits

Water. You can touch it, but you can't hold it. It runs between your fingers. It flows away in streams, in rivers, talking to itself. In both its transience and its endurance it's a metaphor for time. Rivers change every moment, but they are old – in some cases literally older than the hills. They were flowing before we were born; they will still be flowing long after we are gone.

Water reflects things – trees, the sky – but upside down, distorted and fluid. Peer over the brink and your own face peeks up at you: like yet unlike, pale and transparent. That image could be another you, living in another world, maybe *the* Other World. But *you* can't breathe water. So who is that?

Modern mirrors show perfect reflections. Each of us knows what we look like (or we believe we do: mirrors still pull that sly trick of showing us ourselves in reverse.) But once upon a time mirrors were rare or non-existent. You knew other people's faces better than your own, so if you looked into a pool, how could you be certain the reflection looking up was truly yours? Maybe it was an ancestor's face, or a spirit's. Maybe it had a message to give you. But better not bend too close.

A clear puddle after rain is a window into the ground. You can look vertically down into what appears a deep, limitless underworld. A far, bright sky flashes below the upside-down trees. It's a reversed world, the opposite of ours. Could it be the world of the dead, who are buried in the ground? In spring or early summer of the year 2049 BCE (it makes me shiver to write that, but it's been worked out exactly from tree-ring dating), at least fifty people with bronze axes gathered on a salt-marsh (now a Norfolk beach) to construct a wooden ring with an upside-down oak stump planted at its centre, roots in the air, crown in the ground. This was the circle now known as Seahenge, and surely the inverted tree was intended to grow in the Other World – a real and solid version of the ghostly reflections of trees which can be seen in any pool.

Peering into still water reveals three worlds, the reflected sky above/below us, the interface of the surface which is approximately level with the world we walk upon, and the murky depths beneath. Water has strange properties. Half-plunge a straight stick or rod into water and it appears broken, but you can draw it out again unharmed. We can explain it now by the refraction of light, but the effect must have fascinated and mystified people in the past. I wonder if it could have prompted the custom of ritual damage to swords and spears – bending, snapping and breaking them – before they were offered to the underwater world?

For whatever reason, people have been throwing valuable objects into lakes and rivers for millennia. Archeologists at Llyn Cerrig Bach on Anglesey found 'numerous weapons, chariot fittings, slave chains, tools, and at least fragments of cauldrons, trumpets and pieces of fine bronze work.'[1] Exactly what was happening there, we will never really know. But I like to imagine those trumpets being blown before they were crushed and cast into the lake – the mellow blast ringing out mournfully over the dark water.

Excalibur, King Arthur's famous sword, came from a lake, 'a fair water and broad, and in the midst of the lake Arthur was ware of an arm clothed in white samite, that held a fair sword in that hand.'[2] Advised by the Lady of the Lake to take a boat and row towards the arm,

> . . . Sir Arthur and Merlin alit and tied their horses to two trees, and so they went into the ship, and when they came to the sword that the hand held, Sir Arthur took it up by the handles . . . and the arm and the hand went under the water.[3]

At the very end of *Le Morte D'Arthur*, at Arthur's command Sir Bedivere manages (on the third attempt) to hurl Excalibur into the lake again:

> And he threw the sword as far into the water as he might; and there came an arm and a hand above the water and met it, and caught it, and shook it thrice and brandished, and then vanished away the hand with the sword in the water. So Sir

---

1 Powell, T.G.E, *The Celts*, 178.
2 Malory, Thomas, *Le Morte D'Arthur*, Book I Ch. 25.
3 Ibid.

> Bedivere came again to the king and told him what he saw.
>
> 'Alas', said the king, 'help me hence, for I dread me I have tarried over-long.'[4]

Only now may Arthur depart for the Isle of Avalon in a barge full of queens and ladies clad in black. So the sword which conferred upon Arthur a kind of supernaturally-awarded status is relinquished, returned to its mysterious keeper, before he can commence his journey to the land of death and rebirth in the watery Somerset fens.

Even today people throw coins into fountains and wishing wells for luck. In my novel *Dark Angels*, the well of the fictitious twelfth-century castle La Motte Rouge is haunted by a mournful White Lady. I revisited her, and her friend the hearth-hob, in a story called *By Fynnon Ddu* which I wrote for the Sussex Folklore Centre's journal *Gramarye*. In this story the castle is only just being built, yet both the hob and the water spirit are already ancient:

> The hob hugged his tattered rabbitskin around him and peered into the well. It was a long, narrow pool, lined with leaning mossy stones. At one end a spring bubbled up under a rough rocky arch and trickled out at the other into a little deep-cut brook, and the dark water was full of weeds, cress and frogspawn. A small frog plopped into the pool

4 Ibid., Book XXI, Ch 5.

and pushed through the skin of the water in a series of fluid kicks. The hob stiffened all over like a hunting cat. He shot out a hairy arm.

There was a swirl and a heave in the depths. The spring gushed up in a burst of fierce bubbles. The frog vanished in a fog of sediment.

'What did you do that for?' yelped the hob.

A face looked up through the brown water-glass, framed in drifting clouds of hair which spread away in filmy tendrils. The eyes were great dark blurs, the pale-lipped smile both shy and wild.

'You doesn't even eat,' the hob groused on. '*You* doesn't know what 'tis to have an empty belly.'

The water spirit slipped upwards. Her head emerged from the water, glistening. In air and daylight she was difficult to see: a slanting glimmer, like a risen reflection. She propped narrow elbows on the brink and offered him a handful of cress.

'Lenten fare. That an't going to put hairs on me chest,' said the hob sulkily, but he stuffed it into his mouth and chewed.

A bout of hammering battered the air. The water spirit flinched, and the hob nodded at her. 'Yus. Men. They'm back again at last.'

She pushed her dripping hair back behind one ear and spoke in a voice soft as a dove cooing in a sleepy noon. 'Who?'

> The hob snorted, spraying out bits of green. 'Who cares who? S'long as they has fires, and a roof overhead, and stew in the pot–'
>
> 'Is it the Cornovii?'
>
> 'You allus asks me that.' The hob glanced at her with wry affection and shook his head. 'They'm long gone,' he said gently. 'They don't come back. Times change and so do men.'
>
> 'Was it such a long time?' She was teasing a water-beetle with a tassel of her hair. 'I liked the Cornovii. They used to bring me toys.'
>
> 'Toys?'
>
> 'Things to play with.' She looked up at him through half-shut eyes. 'Knives and spearheads, brooches and jewels. Girls and boys. I've kept them all.'[5]

In Frederick de la Motte Fouqué's once famous romance *Undine*, a knight, Huldbrand, marries a river spirit, Undine, and swears eternal faithfulness to her. His previous mistress Bertalda sows suspicion in his mind, however, and he comes to regard Undine's unbreakable bond with the water spirits – especially her terrifying uncle Kuhlborn, the mountain torrent – with fear and disgust. He repudiates his union with her and prepares to marry Bertalda instead. In a spine-tingling climax, the castle well bubbles uncontrollably up to release

---

5 Langrish, Katherine, 'By Fynnon Ddu', *Gramarye*, Issue 5, 2014, 23–8.

the veiled figure of the Undine, who walks slowly through the castle to the knight's chamber:

> The knight had dismissed his attendants and stood in mournful thought, half-undressed before a great mirror, a torch burnt dimly beside him. Just then a light, light finger knocked at the door; Undine had often so knocked in loving sportiveness.
>
> 'It is but fancy,' he said to himself; 'I must to the wedding chamber.'
>
> 'Yes, thou must, but to a cold one!' he heard a weeping voice say. And then he saw in the mirror how the door opened slowly, slowly, and the white wanderer entered, and gently closed the door behind her.
>
> 'They have opened the well,' she said softly, 'And now I am here and thou must die.'[6]

Water is necessary to life. It has many practical uses. You can drink it, wash in it, cook with it, irrigate your fields. It turns your mill wheel to grind your corn – but it may also drown you and your children, rise up in floods and sweep your house away. Homely, treacherous, necessary, strange, elemental: no wonder that we attributed to it additional symbolic and supernatural powers and populated it with spirits. Goddesses like Sabrina of the River Severn, or Sulis Minerva of the hot springs in Bath,

---

6 De la Motte Fouqué, Friedrich, *Undine*, III.

or Ganga, the River Ganges – still worshipped by Hindus who bathe in her waters to wash away sin. (Christian baptism is another symbolic cleansing with holy water.) For the Romans, the spirits presiding over springs were female, but rivers were nearly always depicted as male, such as Father Tiber, Father Thames, or *Rhenus Pater*, the Rhine.[7] Springs, wells, rivers, all were inhabited and revered:

> In Rome we have the blunt statement of Servius, '*nullus enim fons non sacer*', 'there is in fact no spring that is not sacred', and there are numerous references in dedications and literature to such things as the *genius* (spirit), or the power (*numen*) of the spring, the power of the nymphs of the water, the divine springs, the most holy springs.[8]

Water is a living, splashing, unpredictable thing, and its supernatural inhabitants may either heal you or harm you; curses as well as coins used to be thrown into fountains. The medieval cleric Gervase of Tilbury tells of women carried off by water sprites to 'act as wet-nurses to the spirits' miserable progeny.' One woman, tempted by a wooden cup she saw floating on the surface of the River Rhone, fell in and was taken to nurse a water-spirit's child for seven years. When she came back she told how one day, 'after the sprite had given her a piece of eel pie, the woman inadvertently rubbed her eye and

---

7 Campbell, J.B., *Rivers and the Power of Ancient Rome*, 152.
8 Dowden, Ken, *European Paganism*, 43.

part of her cheek with the grease on her hand, and this enabled her to see clearly through the water'. It gave her the fairy sight, too, for some time later she met the sprite at the market of Beaucaire and asked after its wife and child. 'What eye did you recognise me with?' asked the sprite, and on being shown, 'dug its finger into the woman's eye and went off knowing that in future it could be neither seen nor recognised.'[9]

Whether human or animal in form, water spirits can be dangerous and tricksy. Scottish kelpies or waterhorses would linger by the banks of lochs in the gloaming, tempting people to climb on their backs – whereupon which they would gallop into the water. Scandinavia had its waterhorses, too, known as the *bäck-hästen*. The nineteenth-century folklorist William Craigie tells of some Danish girls who were coming home from a neighbour's house in the dusk:

> They followed the path from Skirret to Ryslinge, which went through the morass. The girls were frightened as to how to get over this dangerous spot, but on coming to it they found there an old lean horse, so lean that one could count its ribs. The boldest of the girls immediately mounted on its back, and the others followed her example, for the more that mounted it, the longer grew the horse. They then rode into the morass, but when they had got half way over, the foremost girl looked behind her, and when she saw that

9 Joynes, Andrew, *Medieval Ghost Stories*, 73.

> they were all on one and the same horse, she was so scared that she cried out,
>
> 'Jesus Christ's cross! We are all sitting on one horse!'
>
> As soon as this was said, the horse suddenly disappeared, and the girls were left standing in the middle of the bog, and had to wade to land.[10]

Scandinavia, with all its fjords, lakes and mountain streams, is home to a wide variety of dangerous water spirits, including the deadly Norwegian Draug who roams the seas in half a boat crewed by corpses. In *The Fisherman and the Draug*[11] Jonas Lie tells of a fisherman who harpoons one of the seal-people and shortly after, sailing home in a storm with his wife and children, is shadowed by the supernatural boat. One by one he and his family are swept overboard until at last only his eldest son is left to tell the tale. To see the draug's boat or to hear his chilling scream is a death-omen, and I used his legend along with others in *Troll Mill*, the second part of my children's fantasy trilogy *West of the Moon*:

> They watched the faering diminish, cutting out into the middle of the wide fjord. The sun was westering. There was a bloom of haze over the opposite shore. The mountains there looked flat and shadowy against a sky the colour of tin.

---

10 Craigie, William A., *Scandinavian Folk-Lore*, 237.

11 Lie, Jonas, 'The Fisherman and the Draug', *Weird Tales from Northern Seas*, 4 et seq.

> 'Look!' Peer exclaimed. 'Another boat.' A long way off where the water and the hot afternoon air shimmered deceptively, he'd seen the dark line of a sail.
>
> 'Where?' Hilde squinted under her hand.
>
> 'I've lost it. No, there – see?' There it was, just a scratch on the brilliance. As they watched, it seemed to blur and vanish. Hilde shivered. *A six-oarer, with a dark sail*, she thought, suddenly cold as Asa's words returned to her mind. *And it flickered in and out of sight like a butterfly's wings . . .*[12]

The Draug shares some characteristics with the Neckan, Nök or Nixie (water spirits are fittingly fluid and difficult to categorise). The Neckan is a shape changer and sometimes appears as a half-boat like Draug, or a half-horse like the water-horse. He too is associated with death:

> This water troll resides mainly in rivers and lakes, but sometimes also in fjords. He requires a human sacrifice every year, and therefore in every river or lake where a Nök has his abode, at least one person is lost every year, and when one is to be drowned, the Nök is often heard shouting with a hollow and ghostly voice, 'Cross over.' These foreboding cries, in some places called 'ware-

12 Langrish, Katherine, *West of the Moon*, 283–4.

> shrieks' are also sometimes heard like that of a human being in a death-struggle.[13]

There is however a softer side to the Neckan: he can also appear as the Strömkarl or river-man who plays entrancing music in rivers and streams; though if you listen too long you may lose your senses and perhaps fall in and drown.

At some point during the Middle Ages, unofficial Christian belief and pagan lore seem to have come to a sort of surreptitious accord: such creatures as the water spirits existed – probably – but they had no souls and therefore no chance of Paradise. Maybe some people worried about this, as it subsequently generated a number of poignant stories. In one, a Christian priest is riding over a bridge when he hears wonderful music and sees, standing on the water 'a young man, naked to the waist, wearing a red cap, with golden locks of hair hanging over his shoulders and a gold harp in his hand.'[14] He knows it is the Neckan and berates him. 'Why do you play your harp so merrily? Sooner shall this withered staff I hold in my hand grow green and blossom before you shall get redemption.' The poor Neckan throws his harp into the river and weeps bitterly, but as the priest rides on his way, green shoots and leaves burst from his staff and white flowers blossom. Rebuked, the priest hurries back to show the Neckan this heavenly promise, and the happy Neckan seizes his harp and makes music again.

Mermaids, of course, are the best known of legendary

---

13 Craigie, William, *Scandinavian Folklore*, 238.

14 Ibid., 243.

water beings, physically at home in an element that is alien to ourselves, and stories about them are endlessly fascinating, taking us on imaginative journeys into another world. (What treasures might be down there, at the bottom of the sea?) They too have no souls, and sometimes they mourn this, and sometimes they don't care . . .

All stories are affected by contemporary concerns. Published in 1811, Friedrich de la Motte Fouque's novella *Undine* predates Hans Christian Andersen's lengthy short story *The Little Mermaid* by twenty-six years. Though Undine is a river maiden rather than a mermaid, Fouqué's story must have influenced Andersen's: it was so immensely popular, it's hard to imagine Andersen could have been unaware of it. Undine also has no soul. As she tells her lover Huldbrand,

> We, and our fellows in the other elements, we perish and pass away both in body and spirit, so that no trace of us is left behind; and when you at length awake to a purer life, we remain, as sand and sparks, wind and waves remain. For we have no souls; the element animates us, it obeys us as long as we live, it ever scatters us as soon as we die; and we are gay without care, as are nightingales, and golden fish, and other lovely children of nature.[15]

---

15 De la Motte Fouqué, Friedrich, *Undine*, 60–1.

As a post-mortem outcome this union with nature seems to me genuinely moving, and here perhaps early Romantic and modern humanist sensibilities meet. Undine obtains a soul by her marriage with Huldbrand, yet she dreads rather than longs for one, saying to the priest who comes to wed them, 'A soul must be a precious, yet a most dreadful thing. In the name of God, reverend man, were it not better never to become possessed of one?'[16] In the end her ownership of a soul proves of doubtful benefit, for when Huldbrand betrays Undine she brings death to him, before transforming herself into a spring of fresh water gushing near his grave. There isn't really any moral.

Writing later in the century, however, Andersen was much more concerned with salvation. His Little Mermaid will disappear like foam on the sea if she doesn't win a soul: as the sea witch tells her.

> 'I know what you want,' she cackled. 'And it is stupid of you. But you shall have your wish, for it will bring you misery, little princess. You want to get rid of your fishtail, and instead have two stumps to walk on as human beings have, so that the prince will fall in love with you; and you will gain both him and an immortal soul. But . . . if you cannot . . . then, the first morning after he has married another, your heart will break and you will become foam on the ocean.'[17]

---

16 Ibid., 55.

17 Andersen, Hans Christian, 'The Little Mermaid', *The Complete Fairy Tales and Stories*, 68–70.

Even though the Little Mermaid suffers terribly, even though she has saved the prince from drowning, she fails to win his love. Faced with the choice either to kill him or face personal annihilation, she chooses self-sacrifice rather than revenge and is rewarded by being transformed into one of the spirits of the air. These also have no souls, but unlike mermaids may win one if they perform good deeds for three hundred years. 'You have suffered and borne your suffering bravely. Do your good deeds, and in three hundred years an immortal soul will be yours.' Andersen's harsh message appears to be that it's a long, painful road to salvation: and there is no question but that he approves it.

Like water, water spirits reflect, in the end, our own faces.

Envoi

Happily ever after

Oral storytelling requires a framework. Anyone who's tried singing or storytelling or delivering any other kind of performance in a crowded room, knows that you have to call for attention before you can begin. That's why Shakespeare's plays often begin with a prologue – a man standing on the stage to deliver a speech about the background to the drama, or a couple of minor characters loudly joking and quarrelling, or a shipwreck with lots of dramatic sound effects – something that won't matter if you miss half of it, something to shut the audience up and get them to settle down and start paying attention.

Just as a song may begin with a chord struck upon a guitar, or a run of notes upon a harp, so the beginning of a traditional story is signalled by a stock phrase: 'Once upon a time'. It's a device to arrest the listener and to locate the story, placing it in a mythic but relevant past. 'Il etait une fois', or 'Es war einmal . . .', or 'C'era una volta . . .', or 'It wasn't in my time, or in your time, but once upon a time, and a very good time it was . . .'

The device is common to so many languages, I think people must have been introducing stories like this since paleolithic times. Classical Arabic stories begin: 'There was, oh, what there was or what there wasn't, in the oldest of days and ages and times . . .' A Bantu tale begins, 'Long long ago, in the days before the animals and birds had lost their power of conversing with humans . . .' Mi'kmaq stories begin, 'Long ago, in the time of the Old Ones . . .' Czech and Hungarian stories begin, 'Once there was, once there wasn't . . .'

And this sort of opening phrase sends a subtle but distinct message to listeners. It says: 'Pay attention!' but it also says: 'Though this is going to be amusing or stirring or exciting, it's probably not *true*.' It says, 'This is a *story*. Sit back and listen.'

So the room hushes, the people attend, the storyteller spins her tale. There's a real physical element to listening to a story. It's a ride on a roller coaster. It's not a bit like reading, where everything happens at exactly your own pace and you can glance ahead, or turn back to check on something, or put the whole book down for ten minutes to make a cup of coffee. Listening to a story, you are in the hands of the storyteller. You must listen carefully not to miss a word. You watch her expression, the movements of her hands. You don't know what is coming next, or even how long the story is going to be. Everything comes as a surprise.

Some stories are short and punchy. Some are very long, so you have to pay attention to the intricate, linked narrative as episode after episode unfolds. The princess and the prince are married, they become king and queen. The audience draws breath – but that's not the end. The storyteller is still speaking. The king goes to war, leaving the young queen in the care of his old mother. But the old woman is an ogress, and when the queen gives birth to her first child, the old woman orders it to be killed and prepared for her to eat with *Sauce Robert* . . .'[1]

No, the story isn't over yet!

And so when the end does come, it is often signalled with another stock phrase so we know that the show is over. Puck delivers the epilogue. Rosalind steps out of the framework of the play to tease the audience. Fairy tales conclude with the words 'and they all lived happily ever after' – or sometimes, 'they all lived happily till they died' – or even, 'if they haven't died yet, they are living there still . . .'

It's getting more conscious and ironic, isn't it?

Fairy tales, contrary to what many people suppose, are not naïve. Indeed it is naïve to imagine that 'happy ever after' – much derided as a banal or smug conclusion – was ever intended as anything much more than the signal that the story is over. The bite of narrative has been chewed and swallowed: the show is done. The listeners can get on with drinking beer, eating, bargaining, gossiping, telling rude jokes, or heading outside for a piss. Beginnings are important, endings less so. The stock phrases that signal the end of a fairy tale do not call

---

1 Opie, Iona and Peter, 'The Sleeping Beauty in the Wood', *The Classic Fairy Tales*, 115.

for attention, but dismiss it. They don't place the story in the legendary past; they undermine it. 'If they haven't died yet, they are living there still.' But how likely is that? And so they are far more varied than beginnings: in fact they are often purposely surreal and disconnected.

> 'They found the ford, I the stepping stones. They were drowned, and I came safe.'
>
> 'There runs a little mouse. Anyone who catches it can make himself a fine fur cap!'
>
> 'This is a true story. They are all lies but this one.'
>
> 'And when the wedding was over, they sent me home in little paper shoes over a causeway covered in broken glass.'
>
> 'Snip snap snout – this is the end of the adventure.'

Dear Reader, there are hardly any more pages to write on and the book is nearly over, so I will bid you farewell with one of the best nonsense endings I know, which you are to imagine being rattled out faster and faster and faster until everyone is laughing – 'And when everything was finished I had nothing to wear but shoes of paper and stockings of buttermilk, and I threw them after themselves till I came to the village of Kill-da-veac and Kill-da-woor, to the little turf bog, to the village where I was born, to the village at the beginning of next week, and I fired a shot from a gun, frisky-frasky, kipinny-kropanax, till I killed the blackbird and the goose and got back the load of thirty horses of marrow I took out of the body of the king of the wrens."[2]

2 Lightly adapted from 'King Mananaun', *West Irish Folk Tales*, ed. William Larminie, 84.

Acknowledgements

Versions of three of the essays in this book, 'Fairy Brides and Bridegrooms', 'Enchanted Objects' and 'Wise Fools' first appeared in the new fairy tale journal *Unsettling Wonder* (2013–14). My thanks go to the editor Dr John Patrick Padziora, who got me to write them!

Warm thanks are also due to Mary Hoffman and Stephen Barber, whose suggestion that I might like to publish this book with the Greystones Press had the cheering effect of a rainbow against some very dark clouds. It's been a pleasure.

Above all, my gratitude goes to all the wonderful people – writers and bloggers and lovers of fairy tales worldwide – who have read, commented on and contributed to my blog 'Seven Miles of Steel Thistles' since its inception in 2009. I couldn't have done it without you.

Bibliography

Ackroyd, Peter, *The English Ghost*, London 2010

Aldhouse-Green, Miranda, *The Celtic Myths: A Guide to the Ancient Gods and Legends*, London 2015

Andersen, Hans Christian, *The Complete Fairy Tales and Stories*, tr. Erik Christian Haugaard, London 1974

Armstrong, Karen, *A Short History of Myth*, Edinburgh 2005

Axon, William E. A., *Cheshire Gleanings*, Manchester and London, 1884

Baring-Gould, Sabine, *A Book of Folk-Lore*, London 1913

Beck, Jane C. *The White Lady of Britain and Ireland*, Folklore, Vol 81, London 1970

Briggs, Katharine, *A Dictionary of British Folk-tales*, London 1970

Buchanan, Robert, *Ballad Stories of the Affections: from the Scandinavian*, London 1866

Campbell, J.B., *Rivers and the Power of Ancient Rome*, Chapel Hill 2012

Carbery, Ethna, *The Fourwinds of Eirrin*, Dublin 1906

Carroll, Lewis, *Sylvie and Bruno*, London 1889

Collins, Wilkie, *The Woman in White*, London 1857

The Complaynt of Scotland: written in 1548; with a preliminary dissertation, and glossary, ed. John Leyden, Edinburgh 1801

Craigie, William A., *Scandinavian Folk-Lore: Illustrations of the Traditional Beliefs of the Northern Peoples*, London 1896

Crofton Croker, Thomas, *Researches in the South of Ireland: illustrative of the scenery, architectural remains, and the manners and superstitions of the peasantry*, London 1824

Cuchulain of Muirthemne: The Story of the Men of the Red Branch of Ulster, Arranged and put into English by Lady Gregory. With a Preface by W.B. Yeats, tr. Lady Augusta Gregory, London 1907

D'Aulnoy, Madame, *The Fairy Tales of Madame d'Aulnoy, newly done into English with an introduction by Anne Thackeray Ritchie*, London 1892

Dasent, Sir George Webbe, *Popular Tales from the Norse*, London 1859

Dennison, W. Traill, 'The Play o' de Lathie Odivere', *The Scottish Antiquary, or, Northern Notes and Queries, Vol 8*, Edinburgh 1893

The Destruction of Dá Derga's Hostel: tr. Whitely Stokes, *Revue Celtique 22*, Paris 1901

Erasmus, Desiderius, *The Praise of Folly*, New York 1922 (1511)

The Fairy Mythology: Illustrative of the Romance and Superstition of Various Countries, ed. Thomas Keightley, London 1850 (1828)

Flecker, James Elroy, *The Golden Journey to Samarkand*, London 1913

Frazer, Sir James G., *The Golden Bough, A Study in Comparative Religions*, New York & London, 1894

Grimm, Jacob, *Teutonic Mythology*, Four Vols, tr. James Stevens Stallybrass, New York 2004 (London 1883, 1888)

Grimm, Jacob and Wilhelm, *Grimm's [sic] Fairy Tales: Complete Edition*, tr. Margaret Hunt, London 1948. German originals 1812-1857. References are also given to the standard KHM (Kinder und Hausmärchen) numbers.

Grimm, Jacob and Wilhelm, *The Complete First Edition: The Original Folk and Fairy Tales of the Brothers Grimm*, tr. & ed. Jack Zipes, Princeton and Oxford 2014

Hearn, Lafcadio, *Glimpses of Unfamiliar Japan*, London 1927 (1894)

Huon of Burdeax, done into English by Sir John Bourchier, Lord Berners, ed. S.L. Lee, London 1882

Jacobs, Joseph, *English Fairy Tales*, New York 1967 (London 1890)

Jacobs, Joseph, *More English Fairy Tales*, New York & London 1894

Jacobs, Joseph, *Europa's Fairy Book*, New York & London 1916

Joyce, P.W., *Old Celtic Romances: Translated from the Gaelic*, Dublin 1961 (London 1879)

Joynes, Andrew, *Medieval Ghost Stories: An Anthology of Miracles, Marvels and Prodigies*, Woodbridge, 2001

Jung, Johann Heinrich, *Heinrich Stillings Jugend eine wahrhafte Geschichte*, Strasbourg (?) 1780

Jung, Johann Heinrich, *The Autobiography of Heinrich Stilling, late Aulic Counsellor to the Grand Duke of Baden etc etc etc.*, tr. S. Jackson, New York 1844

Kipling, Rudyard, *Puck of Pook's Hill*, London 1951 (1908)

Kipling, Rudyard, *Rewards and Fairies*, London 1956 (1910)

Kropej, Monika, 'The Tenth Child in Folk Tradition', *Studia Mythologica Slavica* 3, 2000

La Fontaine, Jean de, *Fables*, Paris 1855 (1668–1694)

Lanagan, Margo, *Sea Hearts*, (UK & US title *The Brides of Rollrock Island*), New South Wales 2011

Lang, Andrew, *The Crimson Fairy Book*, London 1903

Langrish, Katherine, 'By Fynnon Ddu', *Gramarye*, 5, Chichester 2014

Langrish, Katherine, *Dark Angels*, London 2009

Langrish, Katherine, *West of the Moon*, London 2011

Larminie, William, *West Irish Folk-Tales and Romances*, London 1893

Le Guin, Ursula K., *Cheek by Jowl: talks and essays on how & why fantasy matters*, Seattle 2009

Lewis, C.S., *An Experiment in Criticism*, Cambridge 1961

Lewis, C.S., *The Discarded Image: An Introduction to Medieval and Renaissance Literature*, Cambridge 1964

Lie, Jonas, *Weird Tales from Northern Seas*, London 1893

The Little Flowers of Saint Francis of Assisi, tr. T.W. Arnold, London & New York, 1908

Lurie, Alison: *Don't Tell the Grown-ups: Subversive Children's Literature*, London 1990

The Mabinogion, tr. Sioned Davies, Oxford 2007

The Mabinogion, tr. Gwyn Jones, Thomas Jones, London and New York 1974

MacDonald, George, *The Princess and the Goblin*, 1872

Malory, Sir Thomas, *Le Morte D'Arthur*, ed. Janet Cowan, London 1969

Map, Walter, *Walter Map's De Nugis Curialium*, tr. M.R. James, London 1923

Marshall, Sybil, *Everyman's Book of English Folk Tales*, London 1981

Masefield, John, *The Box of Delights: or When the Wolves were Running*, London 1935

McCulloch, Canon J.A., 'The Mingling of Witch and Fairy Belief in Sixteenth and Seventeenth Century Scotland', *Folk-lore, Vol 32*, December 1921, 227–244

Medieval Folklore: an encyclopaedia of myths, legends, tales, beliefs and customs, ed. Carl Lindahl, John McNamara, John Lindow, Oxford 2002

Nichols, Beverley, *The Unforgiving Minute, Some confessions from childhood to the outbreak of the Second World War*, London 1978

Nozaki, Kiyoshi, *Kitsuné: Japan's Fox of Mystery, Romance and Humor*, Hokusaido 1961

Opie, Iona and Peter, *The Classic Fairy Tales*, Oxford 1974

Opie, Iona and Tatem, Moira, *A Dictionary of Superstitions*, Oxford 1989

Otto, Beatrice K., *Fools Are Everywhere: The Court Jester Around the World*, Chicago 2001

Owen, Elias, *Welsh Folk-Lore: A Collection of the Folk-Tales and Legends of North Wales*, Oswestry, 1896

The Oxford Book of Ballads, ed. James Kinsley, Oxford 1969

The Oxford Book of Ballads, ed Arthur Quiller-Couch, 1910

The Poetic Edda, tr. Carolyne Larrington, Oxford 1999

The Popular Rhymes of Scotland, ed. Robert Chambers, London and Edinburgh, 1870

Powell, T.G.E., *The Celts: Ancient People and Places*, London 1980 (1958)

Powys, T.F., *Mr Weston's Good Wine*, London 1984 (1927)

Proceedings of the Society of Antiquaries of Scotland, Vol. 1, Part 1, Edinburgh 1852

Sir Gawain and the Green Knight, Pearl and Sir Orfeo, tr. J.R.R Tolkien, London 1975

Sir Orfeo, ed. J. Bliss, Oxford 1966

Sir Tristrem, A Metrical Romance of the Thirteenth Century by Thomas of Erceldoune, called The Rhymer, ed. Sir Walter Scott, Edinburgh 1833

Tatar, Maria, *Off With Their Heads! Fairy Tales and the Culture of Childhood*, Princeton, 1992

W. Jenkyn, *The Welsh Fairy Book*, New York 2001
7)

ıson, David, *The People of the Sea: Celtic Tales of the Seal-Folk*, Edinburgh 2001 (1954)

ochmarc Étaine, tr. and ed. Osborn Bergin and R.I. Best, *Eriu 12*, Dublin 1938

Tolkien, J.R.R., *Tree and Leaf*, London 1964

Tongue, Ruth & Briggs, Katharine, *County Folk-Lore VIII: Somerset Folklore* London 1965

Warner, Elizabeth, *Russian Myths*, London 2002

Whitehead, Ruth Holmes, *Stories From the Six Worlds*, Halifax Nova Scotia, 1988

Yeats, W.B., *Writings on Irish Folklore, Legend and Myth*, ed. Robert Welch, London 1993